A Day in the Bush
Sydney Region Bushwalks

A Day in the Bush

Sydney Region Bushwalks

Les Higgins and Tony Rodd

Photographs by Bill Propert

Maps by Colin Wynter Seton

NEW
HOLLAND

Published in Australia in 2000 by
New Holland Publishers (Australia) Pty Ltd
Sydney • Auckland • London • Cape Town
14 Aquatic Drive Frenchs Forest NSW 2086 Australia
218 Lake Road Northcote Auckland New Zealand
24 Nutford Place London W1H 6DQ United Kingdom
80 McKenzie Street Cape Town 8001 South Africa

National Library of Australia Cataloguing-in-Publication Data:

Higgins, Les
A day in the bush — Sydney region bushwalks
Includes index.
ISBN 1 86436 428 9.

1. Hiking — New South Wales — Sydney Region — Guidebooks.
2. Sydney Region (N.S.W.) Guidebooks. I. Rodd, A. N. (Anthony
Norman). II. Propert, Bill.. III Wynter Seton, Colin. IV. Title.

796. 5109944

Publishing Manager: Louise Egerton
Commissioning Editor: Fiona Doig
Editors: Sean Doyle, Karen Enkelaar
Designer: Anna Warren, Warren Ventures
Printer: Times Offset, Malaysia.

Cover photograph: Hacking River, Royal National Park.

Contents

Preface

The immediate aim of this book is to encourage walking in the bushland and coastal areas of the Sydney region. It has the more important aim, however, of fostering an informed appreciation of the scenic, geological, and biological richness of the region and of encouraging an active commitment to its conservation.

In preparing the book, special care was taken to provide for the needs of relatively inexperienced bushwalkers and to produce a resource that will be helpful to adults wanting to involve children in bushwalking.

Because the book is intended for people who want to undertake bushwalks on a self-guided basis, the 45 track notes it contains are detailed and supported by simple maps. The track notes are presented in a standardised, easy-to-follow format.

The content of the book breaks new ground by offering walks that are linked to background information about the geology, landforms, flora and fauna of the Sydney Basin.

This book reflects the experience of bushwalkers with a comprehensive knowledge and deep appreciation of the bushland and coastal areas around Sydney. These walkers are members of the Yarrawood Bushwalking Club Inc., which has a special commitment to introducing people to bushwalking, having conducted, for many years, a highly successful introductory course in bushwalking and camping.

All information provided is based on first-hand experiences of the walks obtained during 1998–1999. However, no guarantees can be given that the information is completely accurate. Apart from errors that might have arisen in the course of collecting the information and preparing the notes and maps (despite checks that were in place throughout), both nature and people have a way of changing the features of bush tracks, especially signs. Nor should it be assumed that the information about walking times, suitability of the walks for children, grades of climbs, track conditions, etc., applies universally. An awareness of personal attributes and differences among individuals must always guide the use that is made of the information supplied.

Acknowledgments

The concept of the book was developed by Fiona Doig, formerly of New Holland Publishers, in collaboration with members of the Yarrawood Bushwalking Club Inc. Members of the Club also greatly assisted the preparation of the book. Bill Propert, in addition to providing the photographs, compiled field notes and made many valuable comments and suggestions. Roger Lainson devised and prepared one of the diagrams and also contributed field notes. Other members who helped with the field work were Denis Foster, Warwick Hellyer, Keith Napier and Deborah Smith. Without the skilled and generous assistance of all of these 'Yarrawoodians', the book would not have been possible. We are grateful to the executive of the Club for permitting us to use the Club's home page to maintain the currency of the information provided in the book.

In preparing Part One, we were greatly assisted by Dr Colin Wilkins of the Department of Geology and Geophysics, The University of Sydney. His reading of a succession of drafts of the manuscript was consistently painstaking and his expert input has been invaluable. We are grateful to Margaret Higgins for her patient reading of numerous drafts of the book and for happily putting up with her husband's literary preoccupation over several months.

On the production side, the project was enormously advantaged in having the highly professional input of Kathy Metcalfe and Sean Doyle (management), Karen Enkelaar (text editor), Robyn Latimer (design), Anna Warren (layout and cover design) and Colin Seton (maps).

LES HIGGINS   TONY RODD

All the maps in the books are originals, but have been drawn with reference to Central Mapping Authority (CMA) topographical maps of the 1:25000 series produced by the Land Information Centre (LIC) of New South Wales.
The LIC produces excellent topographical maps, suitable for all bushwalking needs.
To obtain these maps, contact:

The Land Information Centre,
Map Sales,
PO Box 143, Bathurst, 2795.
Tel. (02) 6332.8121. Fax (02) 6332.8299.
www.lic.gov.aumapsales@lic.gov.au

Or visit the Sydney Map Shop at:
23-33 Bridge St, Sydney. 2000.
Tel. (02) 9228.6466. Fax (02)9221.5980.
mapssydney@lic.gov.au

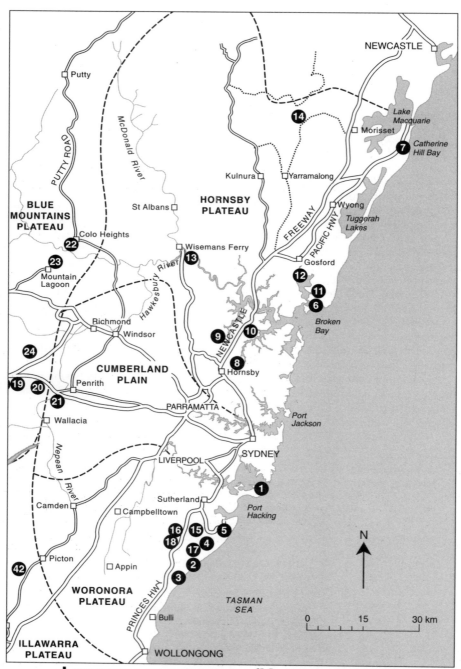

LOCATION OF THE WALKS (NORTH AND EAST)

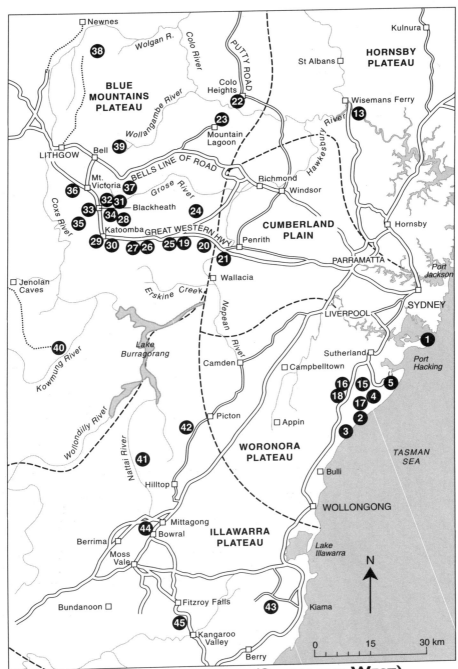

LOCATION OF THE WALKS (SOUTH AND WEST)

EASY GUIDE TO THE WALKS

Good 'introductory' walks

No.	Hrs from CBD	Rail access	Length (km)	Kids	Attractions
1	1	no	10	9+	historic landmarks, cliffs, dunes
16	1	yes	7½	9+	creek and pools, wildflowers
21	1½	no	5	7+	rugged landscape, creek and pool, swimming
23	2	no	11	9+	views of wilderness, forest
28	2	no	8	9+	valley panoramas, wildflowers
31	2½	yes	12	9+	stunning views of cliffs and valley
43	2	no	8	9+	coastal panoramas, wildflowers

Walks for when you are 'walking fit'

No.	Hrs from CBD	Rail access	Length (km)	Kids	Attractions
2	1	yes	11	9+	coastal panorama, rainforest, swimming
4	1	no	10	9+	cliffs, coastal panorama, wildflowers
5	1½	yes	13	11+	Aboriginal carvings, coastal cliffs
6	2	no	6	9+	coastal panoramas, wildflowers, swimming
7	2	no	8	9+	caves and other coastal landforms, swimming
8	¾	yes	9	9+	mixed flora, views, swimming, wildflowers
9	1	yes	8½	9+	mixed vegetation, water views, wildflowers
10	1	yes	11	11+	water views, wildflowers
11	1½	yes	10	9+	water views, wildflowers
12	1½	yes	12	11+	heath vegetation, sandstone cave
14	2½	no	8	9+	majestic open forest
15	1	yes	12	9+	creek and pool, waterfall, wildflowers
17	1	no	13	9+	tall forest, subtropical rainforest
18	1	yes	12	9+	creek and pools, wildflowers
19	1	yes	7	9+	gully forest, creek and pools
20	1	yes	8	9+	Aboriginal stencil paintings, wildflowers
22	2	no	7	9+	mixed flora, gorge (swimming), wildflowers
24	1½	no	15	11+	tall forest, view of river gorge
25	1½	yes	11	9+	gully forest, waterfalls, pools, swimming

No.	Hrs from CBD	Rail access	Length (km)	Kids	Attractions
26	1½	yes	10	9+	gully forest, waterfalls, pools, swimming
27	2	yes	10½	9+	valley panoramas, cliffs, waterfalls
29	2½	yes	6½	9+	valley vistas, rainforest, historical features
30	2½	yes	8	9+	valley panoramas, rainforest
33	2½	yes	4½	9+	cliffs, caves, gully forest, valley views
34	2½	no	7	9+	valley panorama, gully forest
35	2½	no	14	11+	historic track, river scenery
36	2½	yes	5	9+	historic track, panoramas, cave, forest
37	2½	no	11	9+	valley and cliff views, tall forest
38	3½	no	10	9+	historic railway, glow worms, panoramas
40	4	no	9	9+	panoramas, dramatic landforms, waterfalls
41	2	no	13	9+	valley views, river scenery
42	1½	no	16	11+	forest of Blue Gums, river scenery
44	2	no	10	9+	abandoned railway, river scenery, waterfall
45	2½	no	18	11+	tall forest, panoramas

Walks for when you are very fit

No.	Hrs from CBD	Rail access	Length (km)	Kids	Attractions
3	1	yes	6½	11+	coastal panoramas, forest
13	1½	no	11	11+	forest, pristine creeks, wildflowers
32	2½	no	4	11+	valley panoramas, famous tall forest
39	2	no	8	11+	tall forest, canyon scenery, wildflowers

Internet Updates on Track Conditions

This book is linked to the web site of the Yarrawood Bushwalking Club Inc. The site provides regular updates on track conditions and any other changes for all 45 walks, and also welcomes your feedback on the book and the walks.

The web site address is **www.ozemail.com.au/~yarrawd**. Alternately, you can write to the Club at PO Box 113, Bexley North, New South Wales 2307.

INTRODUCTION

This book is for people who want to go on day walks in the bushland and coastal reserves around Sydney, especially for people who are not experienced bushwalkers but who are seeking information enabling them to undertake self-guided walks in the region with confidence, competence and safety.

The greater part of the book consists of track notes, maps and other information about day walks in the region. The walks are located in the foothills and plateau country just north, south and west of Sydney, and in the coastal strips bounded by Stanwell Park in the south and Catherine Hill Bay in the north. The maps on pages viii–ix show the location of each walk relative to major towns and transport lines. The maps also show where the walks are located in relation to the various geological subdivisions of the region — the Hornsby Plateau, the Woronora Plateau, the Illawarra Plateau and the Blue Mountains. All of these areas have their own distinctive features and it is necessary to visit them all to gain a full appreciation of what the natural environment of the Sydney region has to offer. The walks described in the book are particularly attractive, interesting, enjoyable and, collectively, they sample comprehensively the region's remarkable and varied features.

In addition to detailed track notes and maps, each walk description includes information about location and access, the availability of toilets and water, the suitability of the walk for children, track conditions and the amount of climbing involved. It is intended that this information will make it easy for users of the book to:

♦ choose walks which suit their (or their party's) capabilities and interests;

♦ plan walks with confidence; and

♦ get maximum enjoyment and stimulation from their days in the bush.

The walks covered in the book are recommended because:

♦ they can be undertaken on a self-guided basis;

♦ they are, in whole or in part, suitable for adults with limited walking experience and modest levels of fitness, and for teenagers and older children (usually 9+ years of age);

♦ they require as few as two hours and no more than six hours to complete;

♦ they are completely on tracks, some with parts that have been fully constructed or improved in some way (e.g. steps);

◆ they are located within easy access of Sydney or near places offering a wide range of accommodation options (e.g. Katoomba, Gosford and Bowral); and

◆ they cater for people with interests in birds, wildflowers, trees, landforms, photography, and sketching.

A distinctive feature of the book is that it provides interesting background information about the rocks, landforms, plants and animals that will, or might be encountered on the walks.

The book includes guidelines concerning the 'how to' of safe, efficient, pleasurable and low-impact day walking. These guidelines cover such basics as footwear and clothes for bushwalking, the selection of day-packs, how to use simple maps, and how to take care of the environment.

Typical trunks of the Smooth-barked Apple (*Angophora costata*)

HOW TO USE THIS BOOK
Selecting and preparing for a walk

Selecting a walk is easy if you consult the 'Easy guide to the walks' table, located on pages x–xi. This table provides an easy-to-read summary of the main features of all of the walks described in the book. The table also indicates which are the walks to start with if you are uncertain about your fitness, and which walks to tackle only when you become conditioned to day walking.

Having selected a walk from the table, refer to Part Two for a description and map of the walk.

INTERPRETING THE TRACK NOTES

The walk descriptions and maps are largely self-explanatory, but the following notes will assist your interpretation:

◆ The town or village stated indicates the general location of the walk.

◆ The absence of any statement about rail access means that there is none. At one or two places, rail services are limited or certain conditions apply (e.g. the train stops only if a request for it to do so has been lodged with the guard). Study timetables and related information carefully and make sure that the information is up-to-date.

◆ As a general guide, the terms used to describe the walk **times** can be taken to mean:

• 'half day' = 2 to 4 hours;

• 'short day' = 4 to 5 hours;

• 'day' = 5 to 6 hours.

The time listed always refers to a walk from start to finish. Note that these times do not include the travelling time to and from your home to the walks' start and finish points. Therefore, your departure time from home should allow for travelling time *and* walk time. To ensure that you are walking only during daylight, always check the time of sunset by consulting newspaper or television weather reports. A current edition of *The Complete NSW Tide Charts and Almanac*, available through newsagents, contains full-year sunset and sunrise information.

◆ Statements about the suitability of the walks for **children** should be taken *as a guide only* as they refer to youngsters who are accustomed to walking.

◆ As a general rule, water should be carried because very, very few of the streams in the region provide safe drinking water.

◆ Interpret the terms used to describe general **track conditions** using this key:

◆ 'Signposting' refers to any or all of the following forms of signpost or markers: National Parks and Wildlife Service or Local Council destination (and possibly time and distance) signs at the track start, and/or junctions; Department of Land and Water Conservation signs and red-and-white track markers; Forestry Commission track markers and signs; and small metal track markers (which are sometimes coloured) attached to trees or rock slabs.

◆ 'Unconstructed' means the track has a natural and, therefore, a potentially uneven or rough surface. In places, unconstructed tracks have been upgraded with such things as steps, handrails and erosion-control measures. Upgrading is indicated by the addition of the phrase 'some development' to 'unconstructed'. The 'constructed' parts of tracks are fire trails and roads.

◆ 'Obvious' means 'easy to follow' although there might be overhanging vegetation and obscure stretches where the track crosses rock surfaces.

◆ 'Facilities' refers to such things as picnic tables, benches, fireplaces, shelters, information boards, and constructed lookouts.

◆ 'High usage' means meeting other walkers is likely.

◆ 'Moderate usage' means meeting other walkers is possible.

◆ 'Low usage' means meeting other walkers is unlikely.

◆ 'Ups 'n' downs' refers to the number and nature of ascents and descents to be negotiated on the walk.

◆ The following classifications of grades are used: 'very steep'—about one metre or more up or down for every two metres walked (i.e. at least the grade of a flight of stairs or escalators in public buildings); 'steep'—about one metre up or down for every three to four metres walked; 'moderate'—about one metre or less up or down for every five metres walked; 'moderate/steep'—mainly moderate grade but there are some short, steep sections; and 'steep/moderate'—mainly steep but with some short, moderate sections.

◆ The figures in brackets (e.g. 120 in 840 m) indicate the total height gained or lost (e.g. 120 m) for the total distance of the ascent or descent (e.g. 840 m).

◆ Take particular care to locate the **start** of the walk accurately, using the map of the walk, or an appropriate street/road map.

◆ The ◉ icon used in the track notes indicates a spot in the walk that is suitable for a snack or lunch.

◆ Where attention is drawn to natural features such as rock formations, vegetation communities or particular plant species, we encourage you to take the time to read what might have been said about those features in Part One.

◆ Consider the shorter **options** included in the '**Length**' listing in the notes if the full walk is inappropriate. (Almost all the options are covered by the track notes and are well-worth walking in their own right and some are suitable for quite young children.)

◆ 'NPWS' means the New South Wales National Parks and Wildlife Service.

◆ Once your planning is complete and you are ready to set off, **read** the section titled 'Bushwalking basics', which starts on page 2.

ON THE WALK

USING THE TRACK NOTES

The track notes are easy to follow and will serve you best if you begin the walks at the starting points specified and proceed according to the notes. However, you can elect to undertake a walk in the 'reverse' direction. In this event, the notes have to be read 'back to front', so to speak. The segmented layout of the notes was adopted to make it easier for people to do this. Fortunately, the maps of the walks are easy to follow regardless of the direction taken.

Ensure that you have placed yourself and your party at the starting point indicated in the notes. It is not unknown for even experienced walkers to get the precise starting point wrong. This can happen, for example, where several walks have their starts in close proximity to one another.

Keep in mind, as well, that the information in the track notes is based on first-hand field observations made during 1998 and 1999. While many of the navigational landmarks and other features are unlikely to change much over time, others, especially signs, are vulnerable to the weather and the tampering of humans. Be prepared, therefore, to find signs damaged, defaced, missing or changed. Fortunately, you do not have to rely on signs because the track notes and maps are designed to provide all the navigational information you will need.

USING THE MAPS

Best use of the maps can be made using a simple Suunto or Silva compass like the one pictured below.

The maps in the book have some important basic features:

Type of compass most suitable for bushwalking

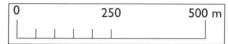

Line scale used to show distances on maps

♦ The maps are drawn to scale; that is, you can work out distances by using a line scale like that shown above.

♦ By comparing distances on the map with the scale, you can easily work out what these distances are in metres and kilometres. The comparison can be made using a small, straight stick, the edge of the compass or even a piece of string as shown below.

♦ Directions on the maps are the same as on the ground. To check directions on a walk, you will first need to orient the map. To do this, turn the map so that the north arrow on the map is pointing to the north as indicated by the compass. The photo at right shows a simple way of doing this.

Take care that you have correctly identified the north arrow of the compass (usually coloured). A simple check is to look for the sun. In this part

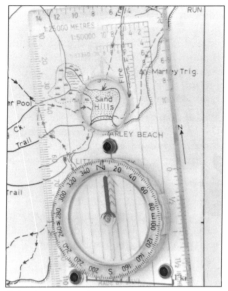

Orienting a map using a compass

of the world, the sun's path is to the north, so that a correctly orientated map will have its north towards the path of the sun.

The north arrow on the map indicates geographic or true north, whereas the

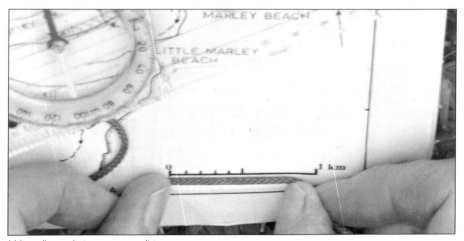

Using a line scale to measure a distance on a map

compass needle points to magnetic north. Correcting for this difference is not essential when using the book, but if you want to do so, rotate the compass and map together as shown in the picture on page xvii so that the north point of the compass is pointing to 12°.

◆ The maps give a general idea about the shape or form of the terrain. This is done by showing a line which links points of the same height above sea-level. These are called contour lines. On each map there is a statement indicating the vertical distance between contour lines. Because this distance can vary, being 20, 50 or 100 metres according to the map, the 'contour interval' should always be noted.

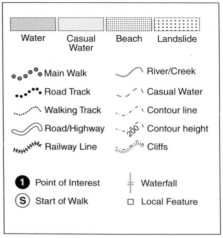

Figure 2 How roads, tracks and streams are shown on the maps

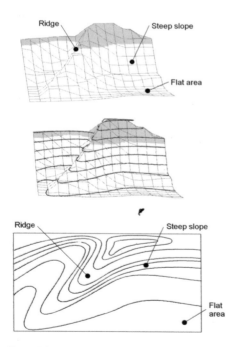

Figure 1 How height on the ground is represented by contour lines

A guide to understanding what contour lines tell us is given in Figure 1.

◆ The maps use a simple system for indicating main roads, secondary roads, tracks, streams and other major features. Figure 2 shows the key to this system.

Part One

◆

ABOUT THE BUSH

BUSHWALKING BASICS

WALKING FITNESS

O nly four of the walks described in the book require a high level of fitness. Even the gentlest of them, however, involves more walking than many of us might be used to doing in the usual course of our lives. If you feel that a little preliminary conditioning for walking is required, just follow these simple guidelines:

♦ Make it your business (and *pleasure*) to walk for a total of 30–40 minutes daily (or on most days). There are all sorts of ways of doing this: walking rather than using the car whenever possible; lengthening your walk to and from the bus by a stop or two; inserting a short time for walking into your lunch hour, and so on.

♦ Find time during the weekend (when you are not using this book!) for a longer walk in the suburbs. Booksellers usually have a range of publications describing pleasant walks around the streets and reserves of Sydney.

♦ Positively rejoice at the opportunity to climb stairs or to walk up a hill! Don't let such opportunities pass; indeed, seek them out. Why? Because there is no better preparation for walking among the ridges and valleys of the Sydney region than to go up and *down* stairs and hilly bits every chance you get. It is the 'uppish' and 'downish' bits of bushwalks that most people find tiring, challenging and sometimes 'character building'.

♦ If you have been physically inactive in the past, build up your walking gradually.

♦ Drink plenty of fluids, preferably water. Drink regularly and often. Avoid waiting until you are thirsty to drink.

Footwear

SHOES

Having appropriate footwear is essential for happy walking. High-heeled shoes, thongs, sandals or skimpy shoes of any kind should not be used for bushwalking, no matter how well they might have served you in other settings. Injured, sore or tired feet can spoil an otherwise enjoyable walk. Thus, choose your walking shoes carefully, keeping in mind the criteria of comfort, sturdiness, support (for arches and ankles), and grip. The last is easy to overlook — shoes with smooth soles or with shallow treads do not cope with loose or slippery surfaces.

In general, footwear made of light and relatively soft materials such as canvas, suede leather, Cordura and other synthetic fabrics is more comfortable than full-leather shoes and boots. For this reason, many people find sandshoes, joggers, trainers and the like good for walking. However, there is now a good selection of lightweight (or lighter-weight) walking boots on the market. These are made from a combination of synthetic materials and leather and, apart from being less waterproof and colder, will provide the same support and protection as heavier full-leather boots.

SOCKS

Another important consideration as far as foot comfort is concerned is socks. Wear wool or mainly woollen socks when walking. Wool is soft and remains reasonably warm even when wet. Walking socks can be a little thicker than those normally worn. In fact, many walkers wear two pairs of socks to maximise comfort — one thinner and one thicker pair. Remember when buying boots or shoes for walking that it is essential to buy a size that will allow room for your walking socks as well as your feet.

Clothing

When choosing clothes for walking, consider their function ahead of style. There is certainly no harm in looking and feeling good in your walking clothes, provided they can:

◆ help to maintain a comfortable (and safe) body temperature;

◆ keep the body dry in the event of rain; and

◆ give protection from the sun's rays.

The trick to dressing for comfort as far as body temperature is concerned is to use the *layer principle*. This simply means wearing several layers of clothing so that, as you warm up, layers can be removed; when you get cold, layers can go on. It is important to be able to regulate your comfort in this way because walking is an activity during which warming up and cooling down can occur frequently and rapidly. Adjusting your clothing 'weight' is best managed by having several warm layers rather than a single thick layer. For example, a thick shirt together with a medium-weight woollen jumper or fibre-pile jacket would keep you just as warm as, but give you more options than, say, a lightweight cotton shirt and a heavy jumper. Fibre-pile jackets can be bought from retailers of outdoor gear and come in three weights, the middle weight (200) being most appropriate for cooler-weather bushwalking in the Sydney region.

For the lower half of your body there are several options. Many walkers prefer shorts because they permit freedom of movement and tend not to pick up moisture from damp vegetation or from a dripping raincoat or rain jacket. Slacks or jeans are commonly worn, however, and tights with or without shorts are increasingly popular with some walkers. If you opt for slacks, something made from wool or a mostly woollen fabric is preferable.

An essential item of bushwalking clothing is a *waterproof* cape, coat or jacket. Shower-proof clothing is not suitable. Apart from keeping you dry in the rain, your waterproof layer can keep out wind and thus help to keep you warm. For many of the walks described in this book, a regular nylon or plastic raincoat would be satisfactory.

Another essential item of bushwalking clothing is a hat with a brim that is wide enough to keep direct sunlight off your face, neck and ears. Caps and small-brimmed hats might look the part but they really do not offer enough protection. For even better sun protection, seriously consider wearing shirts or blouses with long sleeves rather than short sleeves.

What to carry

ESSENTIALS

While participating in the walks described in this book, it is recommended that you carry a few items of food, clothing and equipment, namely:

* rain gear
* this book
* food — lunch and some nibbles such as dried fruit, nuts and chocolate for quick energy
* a lightweight container of water of at least one-litre capacity
* a toilet kit (a *small* roll of toilet paper, some soap or a sanitising hand gel such as Dermasoft, and a plastic toilet trowel (obtainable from outdoor equipment shops)
* a small plastic bag (for rubbish)
* matches or a lighter (for fire lighting in an emergency only)
* a small sheet of waterproof nylon or plastic to sit on
* a jumper (when not being worn)

* a reliable torch
* a first-aid kit.

FIRST-AID KIT ITEMS

Guided by the authorised manual of St John Ambulance, Australia, the Yarrawood Bushwalking Club's recommendations for the contents of a basic first-aid kit are:

* a roll of 5 cm elasticised adhesive strip
* a roll of 5 cm conforming bandage
* a roller compression bandage
* some non-stick sterile pads
* some skin cleansing swabs
* one triangular bandage
* some moleskin and lambs wool
* a pair of scissors, forceps and a needle
* some adhesive dressing strips
* some antiseptic ointment
* some insect repellent
* some sunscreen cream or lotion
* some sting and bite antidote
* one pair of latex disposable gloves
* several sachets of salt for leech removal.

OPTIONALS

Optional equipment includes:

* a camera and film
* an ultra-lightweight emergency reflecting blanket, obtainable inexpensively from camping shops
* a simple plastic Suunto or Silva compass
* a mobile phone (of limited use in valleys).

PACKS

A small day-pack is the most convenient and comfortable way to carry the items listed. Ideally, a day-pack should have:

- a 25- to 35-litre capacity
- a pocket from which you can access small items quickly
- padded shoulder straps
- a waist belt
- an internal frame or padded back, which adds considerably to carrying comfort.

If you need to purchase a pack, you will be faced with choices relating to:

- either flap or zip closures — the latter allows for easier access to the pack but might make the pack less waterproof
- the fabric of manufacture — nylon based, polyester based, Cordura or canvas
- the 'weight' of the fabric — 600 to 1000 denier.

Nylon- and polyester-based fabrics make light and cheap but less robust packs. Canvas and Cordura are heavier and more durable fabrics. Some packs have a reinforced base to help them to survive a lifetime of hard work. Whatever the fabric, choose your pack with the quality of finish and stitching as a primary consideration.

There are day-packs which have been designed to be carried in your hand as well as on the shoulders. These tend to be 'squarish' and, generally speaking, are not as comfortable as regular day-packs.

Avoiding injury

By following commonsense rules, walking along a bush track can be among the safest as well as the most enjoyable things you can do. Common sense suggests that you:

- **Inform** a responsible adult of your plans — where you are going, where your car will be parked, and departure and return times. Don't forget to let your contact know of your safe return.

- *Before* starting the walk, check that you have the right **equipment** such as clothing, water (*at least one litre*) and food that you need.

- Make sure that the **weather** forecast favours your walking plans. Avoid walking in extremely cold, wet, windy or hot weather. The Sydney number for metropolitan and New South Wales forecasts is 1900 155 344.

- Assess carefully whether or not your **body** and your **mind** are ready for the walk you plan, and do the same on behalf of any accompanying children for whom you might be responsible.

- Start the walk in **time** to finish comfortably before sunset. (Check newspaper and television weather reports for sunrise and sunset times.)

- Walk at the **pace** that is comfortable for you. Stop for the rests you need.

Take short rests when you feel a little tired or puffed rather than delaying rests until you are really fatigued.

- Throughout the walk, take **fluids** regularly and, in warm weather, often— don't wait till you feel thirsty to drink.

◆ For safety reasons walk with at least three other adult **companions** — but avoid travelling in large parties in order to minimise impact on the environment and to ensure that a reasonable rate of progress can be maintained (six to eight people is a good party size).

◆ Retain **contact** with the members of your party at all times.

A party should always walk at the rate of the slowest person.

◆ Walk mindfully; that is, be **aware** of features and landmarks passed, of changes in the direction being walked, and of the relationship between what you are seeing and the information on the map of the walk.

◆ Use the **map** regularly to check your progress on the walk.

◆ Watch your **foot placement**, especially on uneven tracks.

◆ Take great care when walking on **wet surfaces**, and especially rock on which there is water or vegetation.

◆ Avoid walking on wet **logs** and **roots** as they can be *very* slippery. Leaf litter can also be very slippery.

◆ On narrow tracks, stay several paces behind the person immediately in front of you so that you can avoid the return of **swinging vegetation** which might have been pushed aside.

◆ When walking through moist, well-vegetated regions, check for **leeches** on exposed skin, especially around the lower leg and ankles, including inside your socks. Leeches can be removed by a flick of the finger, or if they have attached themselves firmly, by being sprinkled with salt.

◆ Be aware of the possible presence of **snakes.** If a snake is encountered, simply get out of its way or (as is more likely) watch it get out of your way. Remember, snakes are protected for the very good reason that, generally speaking, we are far more dangerous to them than they are to us.

◆ In the event of injury, administer **first-aid** and, if necessary, arrange for one or preferably two people to go for help, making certain that they are carrying a note indicating the injury, the condition of the patient and your exact location. *Never leave a patient alone in the bush.* In the case of emergencies, the telephone number to contact the police, ambulance or rescue services anywhere in New South Wales is '000'.

Ethics of bushwalking

Through their Confederation, the bush-walking clubs of New South Wales have adopted a code of ethics or set of guidelines for socially and environmentally responsible walking in the bush. An adapted version of these guidelines is provided here. Please do your utmost to follow them:

◆ Do nothing to mar the natural landscape.

◆ Keep walking parties small in number.

◆ Use existing tracks; do not create new ones; on zig-zag paths do not cut corners.

◆ If possible, use lightweight, soft-soled footwear rather than heavy boots.

◆ Watch where you put your feet; walk around delicate plants.

◆ Do not mark a route by blazing trees, building cairns, placing tags, bending twigs or tying knots in clumps of grass.

◆ Never kill or harm any birds or

Gymea Lily at an intersection along the
Bullawarring Track, Heathcote National Park

animals (including snakes) or allow
others to do so.

◆ Do not feed birds or animals, as this
might be harmful to them.

◆ Do not cut live trees, break shrubs or
pick wildflowers.

◆ Do not take domestic animals into
the bush.

◆ Light a fire only when necessary and
when you are absolutely certain that
you can do so with safety; place the fire
on bare soil, sand or an area thoroughly
clear of combustible material and well
away from stumps, logs, living plants
and river stones (which can explode
when heated); use an existing fireplace
wherever possible.

◆ Burn only dead wood that has fallen
to the ground; do not break limbs from
trees or shrubs.

◆ Do not light fires in ecologically
sensitive areas (e.g. rainforests); do not
light fires in hot, dry or windy weather,
in declared 'fuel stove only' (i.e. not
wood stove) areas, or when there is a
fire ban.

◆ Make sure fires are completely out
before leaving by dousing them thoroughly with water.

◆ Do not burn *any* food containers
(even plastic) for they *all* leave a nasty
residue which will not decompose; all
containers carried in should also be
carried out.

◆ Carry a bag for your rubbish.

◆ Radios should be left at home.

◆ Leave no visible evidence of toileting; bury faeces and toilet paper at least
15 centimetres deep.

◆ Carry out of the bush things that
won't easily decompose, such as sani-
tary pads.

◆ No toileting should be done within
50 metres of streams or lakes, or in
overhangs, caves or canyons.

◆ Be self-sufficient; do not make yourself a burden on others through
thoughtlessness or lack of preparation.

◆ Be helpful and companionable to
those you meet on the track.

◆ Leave gates as you find them.

◆ Respect the rights of landowners and
managers; do not enter private prop-
erty; in national parks and other
reserves, abide by the plans of management and encourage others to do so.

◆ Treat places of spiritual and cultural
significance for Aboriginal Australians
with consideration and respect; leave
Aboriginal relics as you find them; do
not touch paintings or rock engravings.

LANDFORMS OF
THE SYDNEY REGION

Sydney and nearby urban centres, including Wollongong and Newcastle, are located in a region of great scenic beauty, interest and diversity. Much of suburban Sydney sprawls across the undulating Cumberland Plain, which extends some 50 to 60 kilometres inland from the coast. North, south and west of the city, the plain gives way to areas of elevated plateau — the Hornsby Plateau, the Woronora Plateau (which adjoins the Illawarra and Sassafras plateaus) and the Blue Mountains, respectively (see the maps on pages viii–ix).

Although they have had their share of residential and agricultural development, these plateaus are largely covered by natural vegetation and, in some areas, they remain in a state of wilderness. It is true to say, therefore, that Sydney has at its doorstep more natural landscape and bushland than almost any other city of comparable size in the world. This, coupled with a temperate climate, benign wildlife and hundreds of walking tracks, elevates the Sydney region to top rank as a setting for all forms of bushwalking. Collectively, the walks described in the book take in examples of almost all of the natural features for which the region is renowned. These features include scenically stunning landforms, beautiful forests, colourful heathlands and other vegetation communities, and a rich array of birds and other forms of animal life.

Because of the proximity to Sydney of the Hornsby and Woronora plateaus, the adjacent coastline and the Blue Mountains, almost all of the walks are within two hours' car or rail travel from downtown Sydney. Those that are more distant are no more than an hour or so from resort towns such as Katoomba, where there is a wide range of accommodation options.

Because of the nature of the country in which they are located, every one of the walks can be enjoyed simply as a pleasant activity. For many people, however, their appreciation and pleasure will be heightened by some understanding of what is being encountered on the walks — the different types of rocks, landscapes, trees, flowers, birds — and of the ways these are related. For readers in this category, the following accounts of the region's geology and landforms, and of its flora and fauna, should be of interest and help.

Geology of the Sydney region

The region is located in a geological entity called the Sydney Basin. The eastern boundary of the Basin is off the coast on the continental shelf. Its southern and western boundary extends from Batemans Bay in the south, through Kanangra Walls to Lithgow in the west, and beyond to Ulan. The northern boundary lies along a line running roughly from Rylstone to Muswellbrook. The Basin, which is actually part of a much larger trough extending through north-western New South Wales to central Queensland, lies between an old, relatively stable part of the Earth's crust called the Lachlan Fold Belt to the west and the New England Fold Belt to the north.

Between 290 and 230 million years ago, during the Permian and Triassic periods, vast quantities of sand, mud and other sediments were deposited in the Basin. These sediments became the (sedimentary) rocks of the Sydney region. Earth movements, probably beginning about 80 million years ago, elevated parts of the Basin to form the Blue Mountains and the Woronora, Illawarra, Sassafras and Hornsby plateaus. The part of the region lying between the plateaus is called the Cumberland Plain and is where most of Sydney is situated. Over time, earth movements increased the erosive work of rivers draining the Basin, resulting in the lowering of the plateaus and the carving of intricate systems of valleys. The resulting landforms and the associated flora and fauna all reflect in one way or another the rocks from which the Basin is made. Thus, this account of how the Sydney region has been crafted by nature begins with an overview of the types of rocks that are found there.

The most common rocks of the Sydney region are sandstones, shales, mudstones and conglomerates (see photos, pages 10-11). These are called sedimentary rocks because they are formed from sand, mud, pebbles and other sediments derived from the eroding of older rock. The particular characteristics of a given sedimentary rock depends on several factors, including the nature and size of the sediment from which it was formed and the environment (sea, lake, lagoon, etc.) in which the sediment was deposited. Thus, not all sandstones are alike, nor are all shales, mudstones and conglomerates. That is why it is necessary to speak of sandstones rather than sandstone, or shales rather than shale, etc.

SEDIMENTARY ROCKS

Sandstones are very common and can be seen all over the Sydney Region. As their label indicates, they are 'sandy' rocks consisting mainly of quartz (sand) grains combined in varying proportions with other minerals and small rock fragments. Quartz is a hard mineral that is not worn down easily by exposure to the elements. As a crystalline form of silica, quartz yields no plant nutrients and produces very infertile soil. Sandstones come in a mix of colours, ranging from cream to dark brown and mauve. Often, sandstones contain red-brown streaks or bands produced by soluble iron compounds that penetrated the rock and then oxidised or 'rusted' when erosion exposed them to the air.

In the Sydney region, **shales** occur in association with sandstones and are also very common. They can be described

Sandstone with its 'sandy' texture

as 'muddy' rocks because they consist of mud-sized grains. Shales are banded or laminated and can be split easily. Their colour can be grey, dark green, brown, red or black. Many shales contain fossils — the remains or traces of ancient plants and animals preserved in sedimentary rock. For people with an interest in fossil hunting, the Australian Museum produces a helpful leaflet. Another more comprehensive field guide is:

Macdonald, J.R., Macdonald, M.L., Vickers-Rich, P., Rich, L.S. and T.H. Rich, 1997, *Fossil Collector's Guide*, Sydney, Kangaroo Press.

Some shales contain the microscopic fossilised remains of an alga similar to that found in the slime of swamps. These shales, which can be almost black in colour, are a source rock for oil. Oil-bearing shale (torbanite) was mined in several localities across the region. Evidence of this activity will be encountered on walks 29 and 30.

Coal occurs in association with shale and, being a sedimentary rock formed from plant debris, is often a good indicator of the presence of fossils. Coal is recognisable by its (sometimes shiny) black colour. Abandoned coal mines are visited on walks 29, 30, and 38, and much of walk 44 is along the abandoned Box Vale Railway, which was built to service a coal mine.

Mudstones and **claystones** are similar in grain size to shales but lack the laminations. Like shale, they vary in colour between grey, green, black, red and brown. **Siltstone** is another fine-grained sedimentary rock, finer than sand but coarser than mud.

Conglomerate is rock composed mainly of coarse particles, including pebbles and small boulders, combined with other material such as sand, silt and clay. Conglomerates vary in colour from grey to brown, depending largely

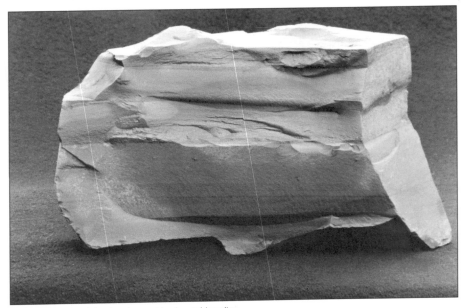

Shale with its mud-sized grains and horizontal banding

Conglomerate with its mix of coarser and finer particles

on the extent of weathering and the presence of iron. The degree of rounding of conglomerate particles can also vary. Some can be angular, but those that have been subjected to the action of water are smooth and round. The relatively large size of conglomerate particles indicates that they were transported by floodwater or very fast-flowing rivers. Very obvious and interesting conglomerate beds will be seen on walk 7 and near the start of walk 40.

VOLCANIC ROCKS

In addition to the sedimentary rocks, three major types of volcanic rock can be found in the Sydney region. Lava discharged from volcanic vents has formed **basalt,** a fine-grained, black rock. Mount Wilson (walk 39), Mount Banks (walk 37) and other prominent peaks on the skyline of the Blue Mountains are all capped with basalt. Rocks produced by explosive vulcanism also occur in localities across the region. These rocks are tuffs and breccias. **Tuffs** consist of sand-sized material that has been hurled from the vent of a volcano. Tuffs can be rich in fossils because volcanic ash can quickly bury land and marine organisms. Volcanic **breccias** are composed of coarse, angular volcanic fragments cemented together by finer material. Breccia is formed as lava mixes with rock fragments that have been torn from the walls of volcanic vents. Around Sydney, the vents in which breccia formed have been eroded so that they now appear as steep-sided valleys called diatremes — about which a little more is said below.

Rocks associated with the intrusion of molten magma from below the Earth's crust occur in the Sydney Basin in structures known as **sills** and **dykes**

(see Figure 3). The most common rock in this category is **dolerite**, a greenish-black, fine-grained rock that occurs in many of the eroded dykes on coastal rock platforms and nearby cliffs. Dolerite is chemically similar to basalt.

ROCK FORMATION

A broad outline of the story of the rocks of the Sydney Basin is provided in Figure 4, which is a simplified diagram of a vertical section through all of the layers of rock comprising the Basin. Such a representation is called a 'geological or stratigraphic column'.

In addition to showing the Basin's different kinds and broad groupings of rocks, Figure 4 indicates when and in what sequence the rocks were formed and in what kind of depositional environment they originated. In respect of time and sequence, it indicates that the Permian and Triassic sedimentary formations of the Sydney Basin were laid down on a basement of Pre-Permian (Devonian and Carboniferous) rocks. In some places, the discontinuity

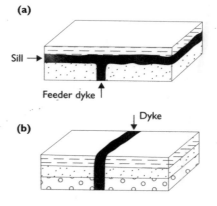

Figure 3 (a) Sill and (b) Dyke

GEOLOGICAL PERIOD	ROCK GROUP	ROCK TYPE
Post-Triassic 205 million yrs ago	VOLCANICS	volcanic breccia, basalt, tuff
T R I A S S I C 251 million yrs ago	WIANAMATTA GROUP	shale, minor sandstone *Environments — brackish and freshwater lakes*
	HAWKESBURY SANDSTONE	sandstone *Environments — rivers, deltas and flood plains*
	NARRABEEN GROUP	sandstone, minor conglomerate, shale and claystone *Environments — alluvial fans, rivers, deltas*
P E R M I A N 298 million yrs ago	ILLAWARRA COAL MEASURES	sandstone, conglomerate, coal, shale, claystone, siltstone, minor limestone *Environments — shallow sea, deltas and lakes*
	SHOALHAVEN GROUP	sandstone, conglomerate, siltstone, shale, limestone *Environments — mainly shallow sea*
Pre-Permian	BASEMENT	sandstone, granite

Figure 4 Simplified geological column of the Sydney Basin (modern river and coastal sediments are not included)

between the rocks of the Sydney Basin and the older basement rocks on which they were deposited is very obvious. For example, near Mount Victoria on the western Blue Mountains, the lookout at Mount York sits on top of a vertical cliff formed in Sydney Basin rock, while the view to the west is of the more rounded, undulating country characteristic of the basement rocks. It was this view which correctly persuaded Blaxland, Lawson and Wentworth in 1813 that they had succeeded in crossing the Blue Mountains. Another good place to see the dramatic abutment of Basin and basement rocks is at Kanangra Walls (walk 40), where horizontally bedded Sydney Basin sandstones sit on steeply dipping and folded Devonian sediments. The obvious discontinuity between the two formations represents a gap of roughly 90 million years and is called an 'unconformity' by geologists.

OLDEST ROCKS OF THE BASIN

The Sydney Basin, as a geological structure, barely existed when the formation of the first of its sedimentary rocks began. During early Permian times (290 million years ago), the eastern margins of the Lachlan and the New England fold belts slowly subsided creating a broad 'undersea' or marine shelf, on which thick sequences of sand, silt and other sediments were deposited. Changes in sea-level and the consequent position of the shoreline governed the kind of environment in which the sediments were laid down. Some sequences were deposited in the waters of the sea that penetrated the Basin (i.e. in a marine environment), and others accumulated on deltas that formed where sediment-laden streams entered the sea. When these deltas remained above sea-level, they provided a 'land' or 'terrestrial' environment for the deposition of sediment and for the establishment of forests. The sandstones, siltstones, conglomerates and other rocks that formed from these predominantly marine sediments are referred to as the **Shoalhaven Group**. As the oldest of the sedimentary rock groups of the Basin, the Shoalhaven Group is placed immediately above the Pre-Permian basement rocks in Figure 4.

The second group of sediments deposited in the Basin includes the rocks comprising the **Illawarra Coal Measures**. The fact that this group consists of a variety of sedimentary rocks as well as coal is important to keep in mind because the label for the group 'Illawarra Coal Measures' is also the name given to one particular formation in the group — the coal which outcrops prominently (though not exclusively) along the Illawarra coastline and is mined around Wollongong.

The Illawarra Coal Measures were laid down during the middle to late Permian era (270 to 250 million years ago). Elevation of the New England Fold Belt, combined with subsidence of the Sydney Basin, resulted in the supply and deposition of massive amounts of sediment. The sediment was delivered by very large, strong-flowing rivers fed by mountain snow and ice.

The type of sedimentation varied across the Basin. In the north and east, the sediments were mainly very coarse, but in the south and west they tended to be finer sand, silt and mud. Many of these finer sediments were deposited in both marine and terrestrial deltas. Forest vegetation from the terrestrial deltas, especially fern-like plants, made its way into the surrounding swamps and bogs, where decomposition was very slow because of low oxygen levels. As a result, vast amounts of organic material accumulated and, under the combined effects of compression and heating, was converted to peat. Subsequent burial, compaction and 'lithification' (the forming of rock) transformed the peat into coal — providing roughly a metre-depth of coal from 50 metres of peat. Somewhat similar environments gave rise to the formation of oil shales. Two coal-bearing sequences were laid down. Outcrops of the more recent of these, the Illawarra Coal Measures, will be encountered on several walks; for example, 29, 30 and 38.

THE TRIASSIC ROCKS

The next major phase of sedimentation in the Sydney Basin began in the late

Permian, but took place mainly in the first half of the Triassic Period (250 to 230 million years ago). Figure 4 shows that this phase involved three major depositional episodes, which geologists have labelled, in order from oldest to most recent, the Narrabeen, the Hawkesbury and the Wianamatta. The rocks formed from these depositions are called the **Narrabeen Group**, the **Hawkesbury Sandstone** and the **Wianamatta Group**.

The basal rocks of the Narrabeen Group began to form when renewed uplift in the New England Fold Belt provided fresh impetus for the erosion of the mountains that were a source of the Basin's sediments. In the northern part of the Basin, the first sequence was mainly coarse and pebbly sediments deposited in alluvial fans — depositional features that form where steeply graded streams abruptly reach flatter areas. Conglomerates formed from these sediments outcrop on the coast south of Newcastle and are among the interesting geological features to be seen on walk 7. The finer sediments from the more westerly fringes of the fans were carried into the south-west of the Basin, which had undergone renewed subsidence (probably in association with the uplift of the New England Fold Belt). Some of these sediments became the sandstones we see today in the lower parts of the cliffs of the upper Grose Valley (walks 31, 32, 34 and 37) and the Jamison Valley (walks 27, 29 and 30).

The second of the Narrabeen sequences began as fine-grained 'sandy' and 'muddy' sediments deposited by streams meandering south-east across the Basin. The last of the Narrabeen rocks had their origins in the channel ('sandy') and flood-plain ('muddy') sediments of deltas that covered the central and southern parts of the Sydney Basin. The sandstones and claystones seen on the lower section of walk 6 from Maitland Bay to Putty Beach are examples of these deltaic sediments. Likewise, further south, the rounded, upper slopes of Bald Hill, visible from walk 3, are formed from upper Narrabeen claystones. These claystones, easily recognised because they weather to a distinctive chocolate-brown to red-coloured soil, mark the top of the Narrabeen Group.

In the Hawkesbury depositional episode, there was a change in both the nature of the sediments (i.e. to predominantly coarse sand) and their source (i.e. the Lachlan Fold Belt in the west). The episode was initiated by an uplift of the Lachlan Fold Belt and an associated tilting of the Basin to the north-east. The rivers carrying the sediments were snow-fed, large and swiftly flowing. They formed a flood plain in the Sydney Basin comparable in size to that of the present day Brahmaputra River in Bangladesh. On the delta, a braided pattern of drainage was established; that is, the rivers occupied many channels separated by low islands of sediments. The sediments deposited in these shifting channels eventually formed a sheet that was 250 metres thick. This sheet became the Hawkesbury Sandstone, the predominant rock of the Lower Blue Mountains, Hornsby Plateau and much of the Woronora Plateau.

Lenses, or layers, of mudstone and shale do occur in the Hawkesbury Sandstone. The finer-grained sediments that formed these rocks were deposited mainly in abandoned river channels and survived because they

Cross-bedding in Hawkesbury Sandstone

remained isolated from the more vigorous activity of the rivers.

The turbulent waters surging along the river channels produced 'pressure waves', which moulded the sand into dunes. The upstream slope of the dunes was relatively gentle, whereas the lee or downstream slope fell away sharply. On the steeper downstream slope, the sand and finer sediments often formed discrete layers. These inclined layers, known as '**cross-beds**', are a feature of Hawkesbury Sandstone (see above). The general direction of incline of the cross-beds in the Hawkesbury Sandstone is towards the north-east, indicating that the direction of flow of the ancient rivers was from south-west to north-east. The sustained deposition of relatively uniform, sandy sediments during periods of 'mega' flooding has seen the formation of almost structureless (without bedding planes or other features) or **massive sandstone**, which is sometimes tens of metres thick.

Slower flowing currents or water disturbed by the wind created miniature dunes that have been preserved as 'ripple marks' on many rock surfaces. During some episodes of increased river flow, gravelly or pebbly material was deposited and became distinct **lenses** in the sandstone. As these gravels are exposed and weathered, the sands and silts that were deposited with them tend to be removed or 'winnowed' away more quickly, leaving lines of pebbles clearly protruding from the rock.

The Wianamatta Group of rocks consists predominantly of shales and mudstones. The rocks of this group are found more or less in the centre of the

Basin. The sediments of which they are composed — mainly fine clays and muds — were deposited in a range of isolated shallow-water environments such as lakes, marshes and coastal lagoons. Almost as soon as deposition of the Wianamatta Group was completed, however, an uplift increased the (rejuvenated) vigour of the streams that drained them, with the result that the soft Wianamatta shales were rapidly eroded. Only a fraction of their former thickness now survives, mainly in the central part of the Basin (on the Cumberland Plain and in patches on the Illawarra Plateau and the Lower Blue Mountains).

LATER ROCK-FORMING EVENTS

The most recent chapter in the story of the rocks of the Sydney Basin extends over the 200 million years since the end of the Triassic Period. As indicated in Figure 4, the major rock-forming events during this period were associated with vulcanism. In two separate episodes, rocks of volcanic origin were formed in the Basin. The first occurred about 200 million years ago and resulted in the formation of valley **diatremes** — volcanic vents that were formerly occupied by lava and volcanic breccia. Because the volcanic material was more susceptible to chemical weathering, it has been removed from the vents leaving a valley in which the soil is especially fertile. Euroka Clearing and Murphys Glen in the Lower Blue Mountains are examples. Walk 10 passes close to Campbells Crater, which is a small diatreme.

The second episode of vulcanism occurred only 14.5 to 17.5 million years ago. Lava from a single vent or several vents spread over an area (how big is not certain) of the Sydney Basin. This lava might have formed a sheet of basalt or it might have occupied valleys and formed tongues of basalt. In any event, only remnants of this basalt remain as patches on the tops of the higher points of the Blue Mountains such as Mount Tomah, Mount Wilson and Mount Banks (walks 37, 39). The richer soils in these localities support more luxuriant vegetation, including temperate rainforest, than is found on the surrounding sandstone.

FROM ROCKS TO LANDFORMS

While the rocks are the 'raw materials' of the Sydney Basin landforms, the wonderful scenery we see there today also reflects the way those materials have been worked on by the forces of the Earth's crust (tectonic forces) and the processes of weathering and erosion. The scenery also reflects the way vegetation and wildlife have adapted to, and to some degree modified, the landforms and soils that these forces and processes have produced. Broadly speaking, the landforms of the Sydney Basin are the product of two complementary processes: uplift of the layers of rocks, and the wearing down of the rock by weathering and erosion.

Uplift

Although they have escaped major tectonic events, the rocks of the Sydney Basin have not rested undisturbed since they were laid down. An obvious indication of this is the escarpment of the Blue Mountains Plateau above the Nepean/Hawkesbury River. Geologically speaking, this escarpment is a **monocline** (the Lapstone Monocline), which is a bend in otherwise horizontal or near-horizontal beds of rock. Adjacent to and associated with the monocline are fault planes; that is, fractures over which there has been displacement of rock. Just west of Kurrajong Heights on the Bells Line of Road, Cut Rock, a west-facing, steeply dipping slope, is passed. The face of Cut Rock is part of a series in a north–south-trending fault which runs for over 100 kilometres. Uplift and deformation are evident, also, in the way the Basin rises to the north (the Hornsby Plateau), the south (the Woronora, Illawarra and Sassafras plateaus) and to the west (the Blue Mountains) of the Cumberland Plain.

There is some uncertainty about just when the plateaus of the Basin were uplifted and deformation-forming features such as the Lapstone Monocline took place. The general view today is that the uplift(s) began between 90 and 60 million years ago, and they might have accompanied crustal stretching and displacement associated with the formation of the Tasman Sea depression, and/or they might have been the product of isostatic rebound — the 'bouncing back' of part of the Earth's surface as the weight of a mountain mass is removed by erosion. There could have been either several separate events or else a continual uplift. Whatever the exact mechanism, significant elevation of the Blue Mountains and other plateaus was achieved by about 40 million years ago. The effects of this uplift on the rock sequences of the Sydney Basin are illustrated in Figures 5 and 6. Figure 5 represents an east–west section through the Basin, and Figure 6 a section running north–south, more or less along the coast.

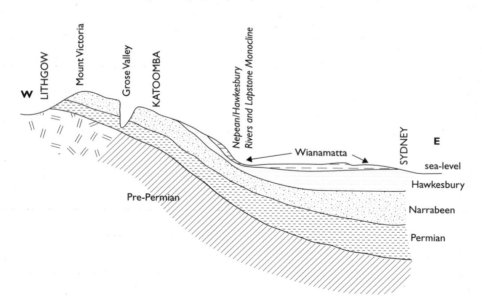

Figure 5 Sketch of an east–west section across the Sydney Basin (After T. Langford-Smith, 1976, *Blue Mountains Excursion 13B*, 25th International Geological Congress, Sydney)

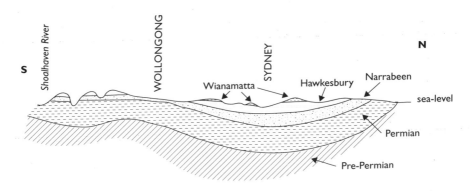

Figure 6 Sketch of a north–south section across the Sydney Basin (after Langford-Smith, 1976)

Both figures show that a significant effect of the uplift was to bring older rocks nearer to the surface at the Basin's northern, southern and westerly margins. That is why Permian coal outcrops are passed on walks located near the margins such as walk 7 (north) and walks 29, 30 and 40 (west), and not on walks on the Hornsby Plateau or Lower Blue Mountains. It also explains why Narrabeen sandstones are exposed in the giant cliff faces of the Upper Blue Mountains (walks 27 to 39), but not in the cliffs and rock outcrops on the plateau further east (walks 19 to 25). In the southern part of the Basin (beyond Wollongong and the Illawarra Plateau), the country that has been uplifted consists mainly of Permian marine sequences (see Figure 6). The valleys formed in the inter-bedded sandstones, claystones, siltstones and conglomerates of these sequences tend to be very strongly benched or tiered and, hence, different in profile to valleys elsewhere in the region. For example, the slopes above Kangaroo Valley (walk 45), exhibit this tiered profile, having two lines of sandstone

cliffs (at the top and at an intermediate level) alternating with gentler slopes of softer sediments.

Figures 5 and 6 help to explain why there are such interesting differences in landform, scenery and wildlife across the Sydney region. A basic factor responsible for these differences is the nature of, and variation in rock type from one area to another. Figure 7 (page 20) provides a 'bird's-eye' view of the patterns of, and differences in, the distribution of rock types throughout the Sydney region.

Another interesting point made evident in Figure 5 is that, in the major valleys of the Upper Blue Mountains (represented in Figure 5 by that of the Grose Valley), early Permian marine rocks and coal measures are exposed, as well as rocks of the Narrabeen and Hawkesbury sequences. This means that to look into the Grose Valley is to survey rocks formed over a time span of 280 to 290 million years. In the base of the Jamison and Megalong valleys, the rocks are 100 million years older.

One likely consequence of the tectonic stresses generated by uplift

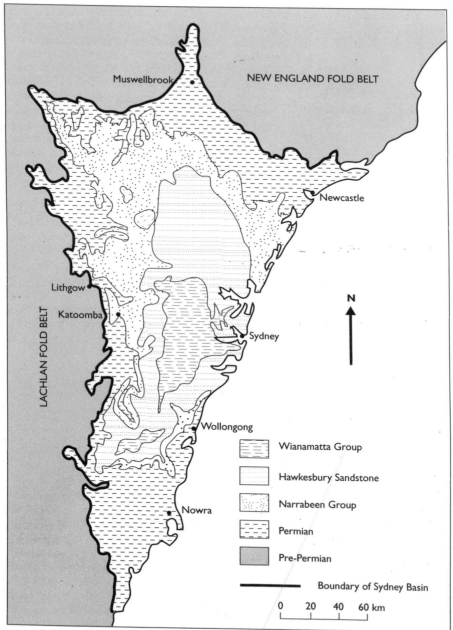

Figure 7 General distribution of major rock types in the Sydney Basin (after G.H. Packham (ed.), 1969, 'The Geology of New South Wales', *Journal of the Geological Society of Australia*, 16(1): 654

and warping is the extensive cracking or **jointing** which is evident in the sandstones of the region. The cracking might also have occurred when the stress in underlying rocks was relieved by the erosion of overlying material. Unlike a fault, the rock on either side of a joint plane has undergone no displacement. Jointing is an important factor in weathering and the mechanical disintegration of rocks and in permitting water to permeate sedimentary beds. On cliff faces, joints appear as cracks, sometimes quite narrow, but are often well on their way to becoming gullies or ramps. On marine rock platforms, they are often marked by what seem like thin strips of rusted iron (walks 5 and 7). This effect is the result of iron compounds entering sandstones and being deposited along a joint plane and then oxidising as erosion exposes the compounds to the air.

Marine platforms are also a good place to see joints that have been intruded or occupied by molten lava to form a dyke. Weathering may erode the lava in a dyke more quickly than the surrounding sandstone, resulting in the formation of a channel, 'gutter' or inlet. Eroded dykes can be seen on the rock platforms around Captain Cook's Landing Place at Kurnell (walk 1). On many of the walks, for example walks 27, 33, 34, 36, 39, you will actually pass through gullies which almost certainly formed in joints, and on walk 38, the track goes through a joint that has widened, possibly as a result of the activity of the nearby stream.

WEATHERING AND EROSION

The elevation of the Sydney Basin plateaus set the stage for their erosion and dissection, which continues today.

We know that an enormous amount of material has been removed from the Basin by erosion. In relation to the Lower Blue Mountains Plateau and the Cumberland Plain, for example, it has been estimated that rock to a depth of at least several hundred metres, and possibly up to a kilometre, has been removed.

Before uplift, the Basin was drained and eroded by several major river systems. Uplift intensified erosion with some rivers, such as the Nepean/ Hawkesbury, maintaining their pattern of drainage and erosion because their down-cutting kept pace with the uplift. One curious result is Nepean Gorge. It is curious because at the upstream end of the gorge the river enters the escarpment created by the Lapstone Monocline, and at the downstream end leaves it. Normally, rivers go around mountains and not through them. The Nepean is no different, but its gorge is simply a stretch where it has maintained its original course during the uplift. The northern end of the gorge can be seen clearly from the M4 motorway at the Nepean River Bridge.

Erosion was also intensified by the creation of new drainage patterns on the plateaus as streams exploited lines of weakness such as joints and faults. Streams on the plateaus surfaces characteristically begin in broad, gently sloping **headwater valleys** of slight gradient. The small catchment areas and gentle gradients of these streams means that they have limited capacity to transport water and sediment. The relatively impermeable nature of shale and claystone beds occurring in valleys has led to the development of swampy conditions in many localities. These upland swamps are usually covered in

The spectacular Govetts Leap Falls,
Blue Mountains National Park

Blackheath (walk 31), Katoomba Falls (walk 29) and Wentworth Falls (walk 27), or at gullies breaching the cliff line. Some of the longer and steeper gullies, like the Valley of the Waters at Wentworth Falls (walk 27), feature a succession of waterfalls and cascades. Even on streams with a comparatively low overall gradient, waterfalls occur, their location usually indicating the presence of an outcrop of harder rock. Walks 12 and 14 on the Hornsby Plateau, walk 15 on the Woronora Plateau and walks 25 and 26 on the Blue Mountains all visit waterfalls of this nature.

On the Narrabeen sandstones of the Upper and northern Blue Mountains, many headwater valleys give way to deep 'slot valleys' or **canyons**, the locations of which have been controlled largely by joints. The canyons have been incised by water, rotating sand, gravel and boulders in **potholes** in the beds of streams. Every stream has potholes, some of which can be metres wide and deep. In canyons, evidence of this abrasion process is seen in the many swirl holes along their floors and in the semicircular grooving on their otherwise vertical walls. Because they are usually very confined, canyons tend to be places with little light. Canyons will be seen on walks 34 and 39.

High cliffs and deeper valleys are undoubtedly landforms that most immediately catch the eye. The cliffs of the Narrabeen Group that edge the Jamison Valley at Katoomba are 230 metres high, while some of the cliffs of the Grose Valley are 300 metres high.

The cliffs owe their existence to the high resistance to weathering of the rocks of which they are composed and to the widespread fracturing of the

sedgeland and heath and are virtually treeless. Walks 3, 31 and 37 offer close-hand inspection of headwater valleys and upland swamps.

Where, in deeper valley systems, down-cutting of headwater valleys and canyons has not matched that of the main stream, the headwater valleys and canyons have been left 'hanging'. **Hanging valleys** formed in this way are to be seen on many of the walks. The first part of walk 31, for example, is spent in a hanging valley, while the hanging valley occupied by Fortress Creek is passed on walk 28 and is part of the impressive panorama seen on walks 31 and 32.

Headwater valleys often terminate at high **waterfalls** such as Govetts Leap at

rocks along **joint planes**. The joint planes are more or less vertical and, with the horizontal bedding planes of the sandstones, divide the rocks into blocks. Beds of softer shales, claystones and coal measures occur in and beneath the Hawkesbury and Narrabeen sandstones. When water reaches these beds, erosion occurs laterally and quite rapidly, so that the overlying sandstones are undercut. Inevitably, the undercut sandstone blocks lose their stability and break away outwards. Many of the walks in this book provide opportunities to see dramatic examples of rock **overhangs** produced by undercutting, and of rock-fall debris. Walk 29 actually crosses the debris of relatively recent (1931–1932) rock falls near Katoomba.

Occasionally, large blocks glide down

Split Rock, Newnes Railway Tunnel walk, Wollemi National Park

an outward-dipping plane away from the cliffs and are then shaped by erosion into a **pinnacle**. See walk 32 for an example. In addition, pinnacles like the Three Sisters and Orphan Rock at Katoomba (walks 29 and 30) and the Pulpit Rock at Blackheath (walk 31), are the result of the concentration of erosion along joint planes.

The rate of retreat of cliffs is interesting to contemplate. Studies done in the Illawarra district, for example, suggest that even where there are considerable amounts of softer rock beneath sandstone, the rate of retreat is less than 200 metres per million years.

The sandstone cliffs of the Sydney region contain many shallow **caves**. It is thought that these caves have been formed by the combined action of water and wind. Water, especially if it contains dissolved salts, breaks down the cement holding the rock particles together. Particles are also dislodged by the abrasive action of debris-laden wind. The **honeycomb** effect in some caves is a particularly interesting manifestation of these processes. Pindar Cave (walk 12) contains spectacular examples of honeycomb weathering. Water freezing in cracks and joints might also play a part in cave formation in some of the higher and colder parts of the region. Some of the more conveniently accessible caves in the region were used by Aboriginal Australians and carry evidence of their presence, such as the stencil paintings in the Red Hands Cave (walk 20). Other Aboriginal cultural legacies in the region are carvings on rock platforms, examples of which are seen on walks 5 and 11.

Although quite sheer, the sandstone cliffs of the Sydney region are not

A pinnacle of the Ruined Castle,
Blue Mountains National Park

stone contains extensive ironstone bands. The ironstone bands conspire with bedding planes in the sandstone to produce a landscape of pagoda-shaped rocks and rocks sculpted into platforms, pedestals, recesses, arches and a multitude of other creations. The description of 'garden of stone' is aptly applied to this scenery.

The nature of the valleys in the plateaus of the Sydney region depends largely on the types of rocks that the rivers or creeks have exposed. Where rivers are still carving their way through Hawkesbury Sandstone, for example, and underlying softer sediments have not been exposed, valleys tend to have a V-shaped cross section. In the valleys such as the Grose, Jamison and Nattai (walk 41), where softer Coal Measure sediments have been breached and there has been undercutting of the sandstone, the valleys have more of a U–V profile. The vertical cliffs make up the U, and the gentler slopes beneath, the V. In the valleys of the Upper Blue Mountains, these lower slopes are formed from Permian marine as well as Coal Measure sequences. The erosion of this mix of harder and softer sediments produces a benched or stepped profile. Vegetation and debris from cliff erosion usually obscures the benching, but some evidence of it appears towards the base of the Grose and Jamison valleys — especially after fire has cleared some vegetation. Look for lines of shallow cliffs among the trees.

Another interesting landscape feature to be observed in the larger Blue Mountains area is the downstream narrowing of rivers. Rivers normally widen from source to mouth. The Grose and some other mountain rivers narrow into **bottlenecks** in the vicinity

devoid of vegetation. Lines of ferns, sedges, shrubs and even small trees are present on many cliff faces. These lines of vegetation, which often seem to be 'hanging' on the cliff face, mark lenses, or layers, of shale in the sandstone. Water moving through the sandstone is channelled along the impermeable shale to the face of the cliff, where it emerges as a spring or **soak**. The locally wetter conditions produced in this way, coupled with the presence of clayey soil from the shales, allow vegetation to be established and sometimes to form a plant community known as a **hanging swamp**. Splendid examples of hanging swamps can be seen on walks 29 and 31.

In the part of the northern Blue Mountains visited by walk 38, the sand-of the Lapstone Monocline. In its upper reaches, the Grose Valley is up to three kilometres wide. At the Monocline, where it is still cutting its way through the dipping Hawkesbury Sandstones and its bed is still well above the softer shales, it is only 500 metres wide and has steep unbenched sides (walk 24). Another example of a bottlenecked valley occurring in the same way is that of the Colo River (walk 22).

Many of the gentler valley slopes below the sandstone cliffs are covered with sandier or clayey soils, rocks and leaf litter. The slopes tend to extend from the base of the main cliffs all the way to the streams' beds. Erosion of these slopes is mainly by the action of water and increases when there is higher-than-normal rainfall and when the vegetation cover is destroyed by fire. The streams at the bottoms of the valleys are often lined with large water-smoothed sandstone boulders and occasionally pockets of gravelly sand. A highlight of walk 22 is a visit to one such pocket on the Colo River.

As has been noted, fire and rainfall play a major role in the erosion of valley slopes. But other agents are known to contribute. The mounds created by cicadas, ants, earthworms and termites enhance soil removal by rain-wash. The Superb Lyrebird is thought to be an erosion agent in its habitat — the slopes of rainforests and tall eucalypt forests. A forager of the forest floor, this lyrebird is equipped with formidable, clawed feet. It excavates extensively in its search for food and in constructing mounds for display purposes. The average turnover of debris by the lyrebird has been estimated at 63 tonnes per hectare per year.

On the coastal margin of the Sydney region, the sea has been a major agent in the shaping of the landscape. As a consequence of uplifts and changes in the sea's perimeter, the location of this margin has changed many times. About 18 000 years ago, for example, during a period of polar icecap expansion (a 'glacial maximum'), the coastline was about 20 kilometres east of where it is today. The climatic warming and icecap retreat which followed caused a rise in sea-level. In fact, 6500 years ago the sea-level along the Basin was one to two metres above its present level, but it has since fallen to the level we have today. There are notable consequences of this falling and rising of sea-levels in the recent geological history of the Sydney Basin. First, with falling sea-levels, the lower parts of the valleys were deepened by erosion. Second, as levels rose again, these deepened valleys were occupied by the sea to become **rias** or 'drowned river' valleys. Sydney Harbour, Broken Bay (walks 8 to 12) and Port Hacking (walk 5) are all examples of this.

Where sea encounters land, it sets about 'smoothing' the coastline by cutting back promontories and filling-in bays and inlets. This work is done by waves and currents. Much but not all of the work of waves is destructive in nature; whereas currents, often in conjunction with the wind, play a major role in constructing beaches, dunes, spits, sand bars and **tombolas.** A **tombola** is a spit joining an island to the coast or to another island (e.g. at Moonee Beach, walk 7). Beaches and dunes are commonly built across the openings to inlets and bays, ultimately sealing them off to the sea. Lakes and lagoons behind the dunes result and, in

Bells Grotto, Glow Worm Tunnel walk, Wollemi National Park

the normal course of events, these accumulate sediments and gradually silt up. The lagoons behind the dunes at Little Marley (walk 5) and behind Stanwell Park Beach (walk 3) are undergoing this process.

The material deposited on beaches, dunes, bars and spits generally consists of particles produced by the destructive work of waves. The rate at which this material is created and the coastline eroded depends on the size, force and constancy of the waves. It depends also on the character of the coastline. A coastline composed of inter-bedded hard and soft rocks, like that of many parts of the Sydney Basin, is more easily eroded than one composed of uniformly hard formations. The south-ern headland of Stanwell Park Beach (walk 3), for example, exhibits much more 'benching' than do the mainly sandstone cliffs along the coastline from

Bundeena to Garie Beach (walks 4 and 5). Other factors influencing wave erosion are the nature and extent of the 'tools' that are used — the rock debris. Waves can be particularly destructive when they force their way into joints, fissures and caves. The hydraulic and air-pressure changes created as waves surge to and fro act like wedges to break up the rock. Walk 7 provides superb opportunities to witness the drama of this kind of wave activity.

As waves erode a cliff line, a **wave-cut platform**, which marks the base level of marine erosion, is formed. Wave-cut platforms will be encountered on several walks (e.g. walks 1, 2 and 5). A short side-trip south from Burning Palms Beach (walk 2) will take you to a splendid example of a wave-cut plat-form, where the pothole-erosion process has carved the famous Figure-of-Eight Pool. Features to look for on rock platforms are eroded joints and dykes and **tessellated pavements** — rock surfaces patterned by a network of closely spaced joints sometimes filled with a ferrous (iron) compound called limonite.

The coastal walks also give access to different kinds of sea caves, including a **cavern** (walk 7). Honeycomb weathering is a common feature of sandstone caves and surfaces near the sea. Salt plays an important role in marine honeycomb weathering just as it does in the honeycomb weathering of inland sandstone. In the case of marine weathering, the salt is deposited on the sandstone by the spray from waves. As the salt crystals build up, cementing agents are weakened chemically and mechanically, causing sand particles to be dislodged and eventually removed by wind and water.

The salt-laden spray that saturates coastal platforms and cliff faces also impacts on the coastal vegetation. For most plants, this creates intolerable conditions, but others have adapted and formed distinctive coastal vegetation communities. Salt-laden wind is just one of the many and varying conditions that have worked to fashion the highly diverse flora of the Sydney Basin and to create the wide range of faunal habitats that exist. The point has already been made that the rocks making up the Basin and the soils derived from them exercise a profound influence directly on flora and indirectly on fauna. Other factors such as the shape of the land and climate are very important, of course. Just how the flora and fauna of the Sydney region have responded to these geological and other influences is the focus of the next section.

For people interested in learning a little more about the geology and landforms of the Sydney Basin, the following could be of interest:

Branagan, D.F. and G.H. Packham, 1967, *Field Geology of New South Wales*, 2nd ed., Sydney, Science Press. (New edition in preparation.)

Pickett, J.W. and D. Alder, 1997, *Layers of Time: Blue Mountains and Their Geology*, Sydney, New South Wales Department of Mineral Resources.

Tessellated pavement, walk 10, Ku-ring-gai Chase National Park

FLORA AND FAUNA

Several things stand out about the flora of the Sydney bushland. First, most of the trees are 'gum trees' or eucalypts (a term which includes the botanical genera *Eucalyptus*, *Angophora* and *Corymbia*). Second, many of the shrubs have a stiff, leathery, springy and sometimes prickly look and feel about them. Botanists use the term **sclerophyllous** to refer to these

Steps on the Grand Canyon walk, Blue Mountains National Park

features and to the way the plants deal with a shortage of soil phosphates. Third, no matter what time of year you visit the bushland, there are wildflowers to be seen. Finally, contrary to the view of some, the bushland of the Sydney region is anything but 'monotonous scrub'. Its diversity of flora is matched by few other places on Earth! Why is there this diversity? And why are sclerophyllous shrubs and eucalypts so widespread? These are interesting and complex questions. In large part, the answers lie with the geological and landform features outlined in the previous section as well as with the region's past and present.

Plant conditions

Agriculturally speaking, the soils of the region are very poor, especially the soils derived from sandstones. Because Sydney sandstones are mainly pure silica, they are very low in phosphorus and other plant nutrients. Moreover, the leaching away of minerals by rainwater over a long time has removed many of the nutrients that the soils might have once possessed. Added to this, the region has benefited very little from soil renewal associated with volcanic and glacial activity.

Sydney's sandstone soils are also very

shallow and, because of their high sand content, water drains through them very quickly, thus compounding the problem of an unreliable and at times low rainfall. Off the sandstone ridges and nearer to the floors of gullies and valleys, conditions for plant life can be a little better. The soils might be deeper, contain more nutrients and have a higher moisture content; but even with these features, they cannot be classed as fertile — a fact early settlers discovered when they tried to grow crops in them.

The plants of the region have also had to adapt to extended dry periods and frequent fires. Dry periods and drought are cyclical features of the climate of the region and have been so for a very, very long period of time. Thus, the region's present-day flora draws its genes from ancestors that evolved with a remarkable capacity to manage low humidity, drying winds and drought conditions.

Dry vegetation and fire go together. Fire was a 'natural' phenomenon of the region long before the arrival of humans; but, with their coming, the frequency of fire has increased dramatically — first as a consequence of the 'fire-stick' practices of indigenous peoples and then of the sometimes ignorant, wanton and careless action of latter-day settlers.

How plants have adapted

The flora of the region copes with the challenges of low levels of soil nutrients and moisture and of drought and fire in fascinating ways. To deal with the low nutrient level of the soil, most plants are extremely economical in the use of mineral nutrients. The foliage of the sclerophyllous plants, for example, contains a high proportion of woody tissues composed largely of carbohydrates, cellulose and lignin. As these tissues consist entirely of carbon, hydrogen and oxygen, they can be manufactured from air and water and, hence, are 'cheap' for the plant to produce in a low-nutrient environment. In many species, economy is further achieved by moving nutrients from dying leaves to new growth. Other species have evolved ways of exploiting otherwise unavailable sources of nutrients: some by having root nodules containing a bacterium which converts normally unavailable atmospheric nitrogen into forms that the plants can use; others by having root associations with soil fungi which maximise the uptake of nutrients (particularly phosphorus) from the soil. Finally, many species from the large *Proteaceae* family, which includes banksias and grevilleas, have shallow, densely packed and fibrous roots well adapted to collecting nutrients that are in low concentrations.

The problem of low or unreliable moisture levels has been managed by plants in a number of ways. Most species in the region have leaves with relatively low water content (i.e. they feel 'dry'). Some plants, including many eucalypts, conserve their moisture or temporarily limit their need for water by slowing down their activity. Because moisture is lost through the tiny openings in the leaves required for the interchange of carbon dioxide and oxygen, some plants have modified these openings or the structure of their leaves so that moisture loss is reduced. Another common device that probably minimises moisture loss is having

Blue Gum Forest, Blue Mountains National Park

leaves covered with hairs or a thick waxy skin (or '**cuticle**'). These coverings often mask the vivid green of the foliage, giving it a greyish-green colour. Very thick coverings are usually confined to the lower surface, where most of the openings are located. Boronias, eucalypts and many other plants produce oils that are often aromatic and might also help to prevent moisture loss. A strategy used by many eucalypts is to have drooping leaves that remain at permanently oblique angles to the rays of the sun, thus minimising heat absorption. In contrast, most rainforest trees have broader leaves that face the sun directly.

Plants of the region survive fires in several ways:

(a) by re-sprouting from underground buds or **lignotubers** (woody underground stems) after their exposed parts have been killed by fire (e.g.

Hairpin Banksia, Mountain Devil);

(b) by sprouting from buds protected by fire-resistant bark (e.g. Old Man Banksia, Smooth-barked Apple);

(c) by re-colonising from seeds stored in the soil or leaf litter (e.g. most acacias, Flannel flowers);

(d) by re-colonising from seeds stored in capsules held in the canopy, opening only when their foliage is killed by fire (e.g. Dagger Hakea and Heath Banksia).

Many plants combine two of these strategies. Old Man Banksia and Hairpin Banksia, for example, also store seeds in capsules above ground.

Not only have such remarkable adaptive strategies as these enabled the native plants of the region to flourish, they have also figured in creating a flora of truly incredible diversity. In many places visited by the walks described in the book, it will be possible to stand and contemplate many dozens, even hundreds of different species of trees, shrubs and other plants. Variation in habitat is another factor that is centrally responsible for the diversity of the region's flora. Such variation is related to soil and hence to rock type. Soils derived from Hawkesbury Sandstones are the sandiest, driest and least fertile soils. The inter-bedding of shales, mudstones and claystones in the layers of the Narrabeen Group produces more clayey soils that are richer in nutrients. Basalts are even higher in nutrients, producing rich, red-brown soils.

The variation of habitat is also related to topography or shape of the land. Topography affects available soil moisture and aspect. Slopes facing north and west receive more sunlight and tend to dry out faster than do slopes with a southern or eastern aspect. Steeper slopes tend to be better drained than gentler ones and soils tend to accumulate down-slope in gullies and valleys.

A further very important reason for the diversity of the region's flora is the long period of geological stability that the region has experienced. This has left species undisturbed and with ample time to evolve together. Even the less vigorous species have been able to find their niches under such nurturing conditions.

Major vegetation communities

Because the flora of the region is so diverse, describing it in a way that is both general and useful is difficult. The task is made a little easier by the fact that plants occur in 'associations' or 'communities'. Species that have adapted to the same or similar environments tend to be found together wherever those habitats occur. For example, on the poor, thin and dry sandstone soils, open woodlands of small Scribbly Gum and Red Bloodwood often grow in association with sclerophyllous shrubs such as the banksias, hakeas, geebungs and drumsticks. In contrast, in moist valleys and gullies less exposed to fire and where soil has accumulated, Coachwood, Sassafras and other 'soft-leafed' trees form a closed forest with an understorey of ferns and climbers. Thus, an awareness of the major plant communities provides a useful foundation for building a more complete understanding of the flora and fauna.

This account of plant communities is little more than a broad overview. Moreover, it is not written as a plant identification guide. For more detailed information, such excellent books as the following should be consulted:

Leonard, G., 1993, *Eucalypts: A Bushwalker's Guide*, Sydney, NSW University Press; and

Sainty, G., Abell, P. and S. Jacobs, 1989, *Burnum Burnum's Wild Things Around Sydney*, Potts Point, Sainty and Associates.

To provide further assistance, however, the track notes in Part 2 contain many references to the plant communities described in the overview. No system of classification is perfect, and this is especially true in relation to plant communities because the boundaries between them are often blurred. Many plant species occupy a range of environments and different conditions of soil and moisture do not occur in clearly distinct areas or zones.

Plant communities are habitats for animals, and the relationship between the animals and the plants comprising the community is nearly always one of interdependence. The removal of animals would see vegetation communities radically altered and unable to perpetuate themselves, while the animals rely on their vegetation communities for food, shelter, water and often for a home.

For this reason the following accounts of the various plant communities include references to their animal life. It needs to be said, however, that as far as many of the birds and almost all of the mammals and reptiles are concerned, actually spotting them in their various communities is not easy: the birds, because they stay well hidden even though their calls will tell you they are about; the mammals, because many are in small numbers and most are nocturnal; and the reptiles, because they have the good sense to keep out of the way. Nevertheless, there will always be birds and the odd reptile to see on most walks. Thus, two other useful field guides are:

Roberts, P., 1993, *Birdwatcher's Guide to the Sydney Region*, Kenthurst, Kangaroo Press; and

Swan, G., 1990, *A Field Guide to the Snakes and Lizards of New South Wales*, Winmalee, Three Sisters Publications.

RAINFOREST

Rainforests are wonderfully atmospheric places — moist, often pleasantly mouldy-smelling, dim and with a green ambience. The leaves of rainforest trees form an unbroken or 'closed' canopy. Often large, rope-like climbers (**lianes**) trail from the canopy to the forest floor. **Epiphytes** (plants which live on other plants but do not draw nutrients from their host) such as mosses, ferns and orchids are common. Typically, there is a variety of tree species, although eucalypts are usually absent. All rainforests occur in areas of high rainfall or in sheltered locations where humidity remains high. Almost as important for the existence of rainforest are soils of moderate-to-high fertility with good drainage, and protection from fire.

The two major types of rainforest in the Sydney region are subtropical rainforest and warm-temperate rainforest.

Subtropical rainforest

Subtropical rainforest is distinguished by its diversity of canopy trees, an abundance of lianes, and the presence of large epiphytes such as Bird's-nest (*Asplenium australasicum*) and Elkhorn (*Platycerium bifurcatum*) ferns. Ground ferns and tree ferns are not so conspicuous. In the Sydney area, this type of rainforest is restricted to sheltered lowland valleys, such as Bola Creek in the Royal National Park (walk 17). A specialised form of subtropical rainforest found along the coast is **littoral rainforest**. This consists of similar tree species as subtropical rainforest generally, but the trees are much lower and their canopies are shorn by salt winds. Littoral rainforest is found on exposed slopes and at the backs of beaches, where it must endure salt spray while catching the moisture from onshore winds. The southern end of Royal National Park has some fine littoral rainforest, notably at Palm Jungle (walk 2), where the Cabbage Tree Palm (*Livistona australis*) is prominent.

No one tree species is dominant in subtropical rainforest, but species to be found there include the Deciduous Fig (*Ficus superba*), the Plum Pine (*Podocarpus elatus*) and the Giant Stinging Tree (*Dendrocnide excelsa*), which has large, heart-shaped leaves that inflict a truly vicious sting when brushed against (fortunately it is uncommon in the Sydney area, but be wary). Coachwood (*Ceratopetalum apetalum*), Sassafras (*Doryphora sassafras*) and Lilly-Pilly (*Acmena smithii*) might also be present, but these species are more common in warm-temperate rainforest (see below).

A notable feature of subtropical rainforests is the high incidence of trees with fleshy fruit. Early white settlers gave these 'fruit trees' rather unimaginative names such as Plum Pine, Black Apple and Brush Cherry. The fleshy fruits of these and other plants have evolved to aid seed dispersal by animals and birds. Not all these fruits are edible or palatable to humans, but rainforests were nonetheless an important source of food for the Sydney Aboriginal peoples. Brush Cherry (*Syzygium australe*), Lilly-Pilly, Plum Pine, and Black Apple (*Planchonella australis*) were all eaten, as was the fruit of the Native Grape (*Cissus hypoglauca*), and the small trees Bolwarra (*Eupomatia laurina*) and Sandpaper Fig (*Ficus coronata*). The latter, a common understorey species, has leaves with an amazingly harsh, abrasive surface, said to have been used as sandpaper by Aboriginal peoples for smoothing spears and other implements.

Warm-temperate rainforest

Warm-temperate rainforest is found in areas that are slightly cooler or with less fertile soil. It is distinguished from subtropical rainforest by a smaller number of tree species, generally only two to four major species being present, and by its epiphytes being mainly smaller ferns and mosses. The trees may be tall and majestic, nonetheless. Warm-temperate rainforest occurs in Blue Mountains valleys and is prominent at the base of waterfalls on major streams. In such places, there is shelter, a high local humidity, and often nutrient enrichment from shale lenses outcropping beneath the falls. Basalt mountaintops may also support patches of warm-temperate rainforest. Several of the walks (e.g. 29 and 30) pass through forest of this type.

Common trees of this community are: Coachwood which has distinctive dappled pale- and dark-grey bark; Sassafras, with leaves that give off a musky smell when crushed, and Lilly-Pilly, noted for its abundant, purplish-white fruits. The bushy-crowned

Blackwood (*Acacia melanoxylon*) and the more slender two-veined Hickory (*A. binervata*) might be common in places, both providing a rapid cover after the rainforest edge is pushed back by fire, but capable of forming part of the rainforest canopy at maturity. Understorey shrubs include the white-flowering Victorian Christmas Bush (*Prostanthera lasianthos*) and the Rough and Soft tree ferns (*Cyathea australis* and *Dicksonia antarctica*). Lianes are conspicuous, mostly being the Native Grape or the Wonga Vine (*Pandorea pandorana*), the white bell-like flowers of which are abundant in spring.

A vegetation community, common in the region and often referred to as rainforest, occurs in moist, sheltered gullies. Because this community is too sparse and limited in width to be classed as true rainforest, it is more appropriately labelled **gully forest**. In most parts of the Sydney region, gully forest is characterised by the presence of Coachwood and Water Gum (*Tristaniopsis laurina*), a tree with bark that is attractively streaked cream and orange-brown. Sometimes the trees of gully forest include taller eucalypts and Turpentine (*Syncarpia glomulifera*). Gully forest is encountered on many of the walks (e.g. 10, 13, 19, 25 and 33). Understorey shrubs include Blackwattle (*Callicoma serratifolia*), which displays wattle-like white pompom flowers in spring and early summer, and the yellow-flowered Dwarf Water Gum (*Tristania neriifolia*). In slightly drier or cooler parts of the Illawarra Plateau and southern Blue Mountains, Coachwood and Water Gum are replaced as the main gully forest trees by Grey Myrtle (*Backhousia myrtifolia*), distinguished by its small leaves and feathery white

Blossoming Yellow Bloodwood,
Blue Mountains National Park

flowers in late spring, and Blackwood. There are some places, however, where Coachwood and Grey Myrtle grow together (walk 42).

Compared with that of other forest communities, the fauna of rainforests is limited. Rainforest is habitat, however, for a number of bird species, especially fruit eaters; for example, Wonga Pigeon, Satin Bower Bird and King Parrot, and hunters and harvesters of the forest floor such as Pilotbird, Lyrebird, and Ground Thrush. Insect eaters are represented by such species as Scrub Wren, Rufous Fantail and Brown Gerygone. Mammals such as flying foxes (fruit bats) visit rainforests.

EUCALYPT FOREST

Eucalypt forest in its many forms is the major vegetation type in the Sydney region. Characteristically, it is an open forest (with tree crowns separated by gaps) dominated by up to five species of eucalypt growing together. But, apart from this feature, eucalypt forest shows wide variation. Thus, the following threefold classification — tall, medium and low eucalypt forest — provides only a very general description.

Tall eucalypt (wet sclerophyll) forest

Tall eucalypt forest occurs in moist valleys and on the more sheltered slopes having an easterly or southerly aspect, or sometimes on the more exposed summits with basalt caps such as Mount Wilson (walk 39) and Mount Tomah. Unlike rainforest, it is subject to fire — in fact, without occasional fires, it could eventually convert to rainforest. The canopy of tall eucalypt forest exceeds 30 metres at maturity (hence the label 'tall').

Just which trees form associations in tall eucalypt forest varies from area to area, depending on soil type and fertility, rainfall and altitude. In some cases, there is a single dominant species — for example, Round-leaved Blue Gum (*Eucalyptus deanei*), apparent in the Blue Gum Forest (walk 32) and along Blue Gum Creek (walk 42). In more easterly parts of the region, where tall forest survives on Wianamatta shale, Sydney Blue Gum (*E. saligna*) and Grey Ironbark (*E. paniculata*) often form an association with Turpentine. On more sandy soils, the dominance can shift to Blackbutt (*E. pilularis*) — for example, in the Hacking River valley of Royal National Park (walk 17) and on the escarpment behind Stanwell Park (walk 3). Several of the tall-tree species are easily identified. The bark of the Blue Gum is smooth above a very short collar, while that of Blackbutt is usually rough for quite a few metres above the base and is often fire-blackened. Turpentine bark is stringy, furrowed and reddish-brown, and the Turpentine's shorter leaves, with dirty-whitish undersides, are also easily distinguished from those of eucalypts. Ironbarks are recognised by their deeply furrowed, very hard bark.

In higher sandstone gullies and on some deep plateau soils, the beautiful Blue Mountains Ash (*E. oreades*) (walk 38) sometimes forms pure stands. On basalt soils such as those of Mount Wilson (walk 39), Brown Barrel (*E. fastigata*) may grow to a massive size. Valleys of the Illawarra Plateau contain fine stands of River Peppermint *(E. elata)* (walk 41).

The understorey in tall eucalypt forest consists largely, but not exclusively, of relatively soft, 'moist' plants (hence the label 'wet') including, in many instances, ground and tree ferns, rainforest shrubs and epiphytes such as Elkhorn and Bird's-nest Fern. Common smaller trees include the ferny-leaved Cedar Wattle (*Acacia elata*) and the Forest She-oak (*Allocasuarina torulosa*) with its drooping pine-like foliage — both growing at times to twenty metres or even more. Tall shrubs might be in abundance; for example, the Graceful Bush-pea (*Pultenaea flexilis*), which bursts into a mist of golden-yellow blossom in mid-spring. Climbers are often plentiful, although they are unable to access the tree crowns as they do in rainforest. Among the more common climbers are Traveller's Joy (*Clematis aristata*), which has massed white flowers in late spring, and Native Grape, easily identified in autumn when its blue-black fruit forms.

Tall eucalypt forests support many bird and several mammal species. An important food for nectar-eating birds and animals is the sugary exudate produced by some eucalypts as a defence against damage or insect attack. Forests on the more fertile soils, at Mount Wilson (walk 39), Mount Banks (walk 37), Blue Gum Swamp Creek (walk 24) and the Blue Gum .

Forest (walk 32) support the richest fauna, particularly birds and leaf-eating mammals such as the Common Ringtail Possum, the Mountain Brushtail Possum, and the Greater Glider. Macropods such as the Swamp Wallaby are quite common in some areas. Where the understorey becomes open and grassy, groups of Eastern Grey Kangaroo are sometimes seen, especially towards dusk. Wombats have a patchy distribution close to Sydney, but at Mill Creek (walk 13) they are often seen at evening around the picnic area. Other reasonably common but seldom seen mammals of the forest are Sugar Gliders, Brown and Dusky Antechinus and the Bush Rat.

Nectar-feeding birds of tall eucalypt forests include the White-naped and Crescent Honeyeaters. Among the seed-eaters are the Australian King Parrot and several species of cockatoo, including the Gang Gang, the Sulphur-crested Cockatoo and the Yellow-tailed Black Cockatoo (which also feeds on insect larvae extracted from tree trunks, banksia cones and grass-tree flower spikes). Of the insect-eaters, one of the best known is the Bell Miner (often referred to as the 'Bellbird'). It is seldom visible but easily detected by its high-pitched 'tink-tink-tink' call. Bell Miner colonies tend to be isolated and are more likely to be established where the trees have been infested by lerps (young psyllid insects). Other insect-eaters are the White-throated Treecreeper, Spotted Satin Flycatcher, Pardalote, Dollarbird (which also eats small birds), Rufous Fantail, Brown Gerygone, Black-faced Cuckooshrike (berries and fruit are also eaten) and the nest-invading Fan-tailed Cuckoo. Lyrebird, Pilotbird, Wonga Pigeon and

Ground Thrush are joined by the Eastern Whipbird and Golden Whistler as hunters of insects and invertebrates in the forest litter. In one or two odd corners of the moist forest, including that in the Bouddi National Park (walk 6), it is still possible to spot Brush Turkeys. Common fruit eaters are the Mistletoebird, Satin Bowerbird and Brown Pigeon. The most common predatory birds of open forests are the Southern Boobook and, in a few localities, the Powerful Owl. The Wedge-tailed Eagle, our largest bird of prey, can sometimes be seen soaring above the forests of the Upper Blue Mountains, and the Peregrine Falcon, which finds cliff ledges ideal for nesting, is moderately common.

Many of the reptile inhabitants of tall eucalypt forests are found across a range of communities. There are a few species, however, which are more likely to be found in moister forests. These include the Thick-tailed Gecko, the Golden-crowned Snake and the Diamond Python.

Medium eucalypt forest

Medium eucalypt (or dry sclerophyll) forest is the kind of forest bushwalkers are most likely to bring to mind when they think of 'the bush', simply because it is the most widespread vegetation community in the Sydney region and covers, in its various guises, most of the sandstone ridges and hill slopes of the coast and mountains. It has a canopy that ranges in height from 10 to 30 metres.

Many different eucalypt species, some common, some rare, occur in medium eucalypt forest. Some of the more common species are Sydney Peppermint (*Eucalyptus piperita*),

Silvertop Ash (*E. sieberi*) and Smooth-barked Apple or Sydney Red Gum (*Angophora costata*), a beautiful pinkish-barked tree with twisted limbs. Others are the Scribbly Gums (*E. haemastoma, E. sclerophylla*), a group of species with greyish-cream bark on which there are curious 'scribbles' made by a burrowing moth larva. The bloodwoods are another widespread group. Both the Red Bloodwood (*Corymbia gummifera*) and Yellow Bloodwood (*C. eximia*) have a distinctive, flaky bark.

The understorey of medium eucalypt forest is remarkably diverse. In most places it is dominated by sclerophyllous (hard, stiff-leaved) shrubs such as acacias (wattles), tea-trees, banksias, hakeas, drumsticks and grevilleas (spider flowers), but there are pockets where grasses predominate. Other shrubs which occur commonly in open forests are Mountain Devil (*Lambertia formosa*), Hairpin Banksia (*Banksia spinulosa*) and Broad-leaf Geebung (*Persoonia levis*), readily identified by its remarkable flaky bark — bright red below a black outer layer. Seen less often, but spectacular in flower, is the Waratah (*Telopea speciosissima*).

In the open forests of the Royal and Heathcote National Parks (walks 15–18) is found the Gymea Lily (*Doryanthes excelsa*) — a gigantic sword-leaved lily with large heads of scarlet flowers atop four-metre stems. Other notable plants of the open forests are the grass-trees (*Xanthorrhoea*) and the Burrawang (*Macrozamia communis*), a relic of an ancient group of plants known as cycads.

While much medium eucalypt forest is on drier ridges and slopes, there are large areas in gullies and on south-facing slopes, where moister conditions prevail. In these sites, the forest is often taller (though not tall enough to be classed as tall eucalypt forest) and tends to have a denser understorey as well. The mix of species in all layers of the forest varies almost endlessly, governed by rock and soil type, degree of shelter, altitude, distance from the sea, and frequency of bushfires.

The flowers of many sclerophyllous shrubs are rich in nectar and pollen (an important source of protein). This makes the medium eucalypt forests attractive to nectar-eating birds such as Eastern Spinebill, Red Wattlebird and various species of honeyeaters, and mammals like the Eastern Pygmy Possum and Sugar Glider. Moister and grassier parts of the forest often support populations of grazing marsupials; for example, Red-necked Wallaby and Grey Kangaroo. Swamp Wallabies are relatively common where there are dense thickets of grass, sedges and ferns. In higher parts of the Sydney region, the Common Wombat or, more likely, its droppings and burrows are likely to be encountered. Another burrower, the Echidna, is occasionally spotted in the dry forests. Superbly equipped with a long sticky tongue to locate and eat ants, the Echidna can escape danger by digging a hole and covering itself with soil.

Common bird species of medium eucalypt forest include the Crimson Rosella, Sulphur-crested Cockatoo, White-throated Treecreeper, Kookaburra, Red Wattlebird, Magpie, Pied Currawong and Australian Raven (sometimes called 'crow').

Among the reptiles that appear to favour drier forests are species of gecko, dragons and skinks, including the Blotched and the Eastern Blue-tongued

Bark of a Scribbly Gum, Great North Walk, Ku-ring-gai Chase National Park

lizards. Along creeks, the Eastern Water Dragon is common, its presence often betrayed by a 'plop' when it takes to the water. Snake species most likely to be encountered, especially in early summer and through the warmer months, are the Red-bellied Black Snake (especially near creeks), Eastern Brown Snake and Eastern Tiger Snake. The Death Adder, once common, is now rarely seen.

Low eucalypt forest

Low eucalypt forest is found mainly on sandstone plateaus and ridges with very shallow or poorly drained soils. It is not markedly different in general character from medium eucalypt forest, but its trees are lower growing (usually less than 10 metres) and more scattered.

A distinctive small tree that occurs in low eucalypt forest on the Woronora and Hornsby plateaus is the Dwarf Apple (*Angophora hispida*). It has broad, stiff-textured leaves and large clusters of bristly buds that open to masses of white blossom in late spring.

The understorey of low eucalypt forest is composed of many of the plants found in medium eucalypt forest, especially those particularly well adapted to poorer and thinner soils. In general, the understorey of low eucalypt forest is dominated by sclerophyllous species and might be quite sparse. Consequently, low eucalypt forest supports only a very limited fauna. This kind of forest can be seen as a transitional form between medium eucalypt forest and heathland.

HEATHLAND

Heathland or heath is composed of low, small-leafed plants that are often densely crowded and tangled together. Heath occurs in two habitats: (a) rocky, windswept ridges and plateaus and (b) broad, swampy valleys or poorly drained slopes. Heaths often form a mosaic with low eucalypt forests because their habitats are similar. Heaths are more common in the higher rainfall areas of Ku-ring-gai Chase, Brisbane Water national parks (eg. walks 8 and 12), the Blue Mountains (walks 28, 37 and 40) and the Woronora Plateau (walks 4, 5 and 15). They also develop on coastal sand dunes, when the accumulation of peat from dead plants impedes drainage.

Depending on the type of plants that predominate, heaths can be divided into two broad categories: shrub heaths and sedge heaths. **Shrub heaths** can be quite tall. Common close to Sydney is

shrub heath dominated by Heath Banksia (*Banksia ericifolia*), Dagger Hakea (*Hakea teretifolia*) and Scrub She-oak (*Allocasuarina distyla*), all of which can reach three to four metres high. True trees are absent from heaths but eucalypts are represented by mallees, multi-stemmed species growing from a large rootstock and forming low, spreading canopies only two to five metres high. In parts of the Upper Blue Mountains, there is an interesting type of shrub heath dominated by Dwarf She-oak (*Allocasuarina nana*), which forms low, dense mounds that turn a dull purplish-colour in winter.

Sedge heaths (or sedgelands) are dominated by sedges and rushes and generally develop on waterlogged ground. Apart from the true sedges (family *Cyperaceae*), Australian sedge-lands are rich in members of the southern-hemisphere family *Restionaceae* — sedge-like plants to which 'book names' such as Scale-rush, Cord-rush, Rope-rush and Twine-rush have been given. Yellow-eyes (*Xyris*) occur commonly in sedge heath, producing pretty yellow flowers from rush-like bases in spring and summer. The spectacular Christmas Bells (*Blandfordia nobilis* and *B. grandiflora*) send up tall spikes of waxy crimson bells from grassy-leafed tufts.

Large seepage areas on plateau slopes and cliff ledges support a distinctive kind of sedge heath known as **hanging swamps**. These might be dominated by the large, tussock-forming sedge Button 'Grass' (*Gymnoschoenus sphaerocephalus*), whose knob-like seed-heads are borne on arching stalks up to two metres long. This same species extends to Tasmania where it forms the famous 'button grass plains' of the south-west.

Many heaths contain both sedges and shrubs. A striking heath shrub that grows among dense sedges is the Swamp Banksia (*Banksia robur*), while in the Blue Mountains the red-flowered Prickly Grevillea (*Grevillea acanthifolia*) grows in hanging swamps. Among the lower-growing shrubs, one of the commonest is the white-flowered Coral Heath (*Epacris microphylla*).

Heath is an important fauna habitat. The flowers of Heath Banksia are a valuable food source for several small mammals, including the Eastern Pygmy-Possum, and for a range of honeyeaters. Several uncommon bird species are most likely to be seen in heath communities. For example, the heathland of Barren Grounds Nature Reserve (walk 43) is the home of the rare Eastern Bristlebird and Ground Parrot. In denser heathlands on the coastal strip and in the Blue Mountains, the Variegated Wren is fairly common. Heathland is a popular habitat for several species of lizards and snakes, including the Eastern Tiger Snake and the Red-bellied Black Snake.

OTHER COMMUNITIES
Fringing forest

Rivers, swamps, lagoons and estuaries often have a distinctive forest type fringing their margins. Such fringing forest is frequently dominated by a single tree species. Two species of She-oaks (*Casuarinas*) are prominent, and their distribution around Sydney is interesting. The majestic River She-oak (*C. cunninghamiana*) is a feature of larger freshwater streams with sandy or boulder-laden beds. In the Hawkesbury/Nepean system it occurs upstream from Windsor and along streams in all of the deep Blue Mountains valleys (e.g. walk 35). Closer to the coast it is replaced by Swamp She-oak (*C. glauca*), which has coarser, darker-green 'needles'. This species can grow in quite saline environments around estuaries and lagoons. The 'needles' (stems) of She-oaks are obvious, but the leaves have been reduced to ribs projecting at nodes along the 'needles' as whorls of teeth.

The other characteristic tree genus of fringing forest is *Melaleuca*, whose regional species are recognisable by their papery, cream bark that peels off in layers. In coastal swamps and along estuaries, the Broad-leaved Paperbark (*M. quinquenervia*) can form forests up to twenty-five metres high, but Sydney is close to its southern limit on the Australian coast. The Prickly-leaved Paperbark (*M. styphelioides*) occurs in various habitats, from mangrove swamp edges to moist mountain gullies.

Another common estuarine tree is the Grey Mangrove (*Avicennia marina* subsp. *australasica*), which has spiky pneumatophores (breathing roots) that protrude from the inter-tidal mud. The smaller River Mangrove (*Aegiceras corniculatum*) has greener, more-rounded leaves and is also a common estuarine tree.

Common birds of estuaries include Little Black Cormorant, Little Pied Cormorant, Silver Gull, Spur-winged Plover, Curlew Sandpiper, White Ibis, Black Duck and Chestnut Teal.

Coastal dune scrub

Dunes formed from windblown sand at the backs of beaches are continually being colonised by plants that are adapted to survival in this very exposed and saline environment. The under-mining of roots by the erosive action of the wind occurs frequently. These conditions result in a very confused, dynamic plant community, with vegetation of very mixed ages. Given time, dune communities can mature to either forest or heathland, but they can remain almost indefinitely in a state where the trees are sparse and very stunted, and shrubs and grass-like plants are predominant. This type of vegetation is most appropriately classed as a 'scrub'. Among the most common trees struggling to grow in dune scrubs is the Coast Banksia (*Banksia integrifolia*), although Old Man Banksia (*B. serrata*) might also be in evidence. On the more sheltered backs of dunes, trees with rainforest affinities such as Tuckeroo (*Cupaniopsis anacardioides*) may occur. Coast Tea-tree (*Leptospermum laevigatum*) is a common tall shrub in dune scrub, sometimes forming dense thickets. Among the lower-growing plants on coastal dunes is the widespread Honey-reed (*Lomandra longifolia*), the grass-like leaves of which terminate in two or three spine-like teeth. The exposed fronts of the dunes have their own characteristic flora, notably Spinifex Grass (*Spinifex sericeus*), which has long creeping stems with chaffy male and spidery female flower-heads on separate plants.

The creeping, succulent Pigface (*Carpobrotus glaucescens*), which is also seen on the faces of dunes, has a soft, sweet fruit, which has been eaten by Aboriginal peoples. Walks 5 and 7 pass through coastal dune scrub. These and the other coastal walks described in the book afford opportunities to see birds of the seashore such as the Little Pied Cormorant, Great Cormorant, Little Black Cormorant, Silver Gull and Crested Tern.

Saltmarsh

Saltmarsh is a treeless plant community found on saline, waterlogged soil around edges of estuaries and lagoons. Only a small number of plant species occur in saltmarsh, and the dominant plant varies from place to place. Where salinity is highest, the succulent-stemmed Samphire (*Sarcocornia quinqueflora*), a member of the saltbush family, might be the only plant present. Another member of the saltbush family found in saltmarsh is Seablite (*Suaeda australis*), which has narrow, succulent, bright-green leaves. In less saline saltmarsh, the dominant plant is often Knob-sedge (*Isolepis nodosa*), a dense, rush-like plant with knobbly brown seed-heads. A saltmarsh community is encountered in walk 9.

Part Two

◆

THE WALKS

*Guidelines for interpreting these track notes and maps
are provided in the section, 'How to use this book',
on pages xiv–xv.*

··

Coast Walks

Although all of the walks in this category are located on or very near the coast
north and south of Sydney, they offer an enormous variety of attractions.
Coastal panoramas are a feature of all of them. Walks 2 and 3 provide views from
an escarpment several hundred metres above sea-level, and walks 4, 5 and 6 offer
exciting views of cliffs and wave-cut platforms. Dramatic features created by
marine erosion, including caves, are visited on walk 7, and volcanic dykes can be
seen on walk 1. The vegetation encountered on the coastal walks is possibly even
more varied than the landforms. Both tall and gully forests are features of walk 3,
and a highlight of walk 2 is a descent through an interesting rainforest. Heathlands
and dune scrub can be enjoyed on walks 4, 5 and 7, and the swamps seen on
walk 1 are especially interesting.

No. 1

Captain Cook's Landing Place –
Cape Baily Lighthouse

*This accessible walk in Botany Bay National Park
near Kurnell features historic landmarks,
coastal landforms, impressive dunes,
heath and wildflowers*

♦ **Length:** 10 km; or walking ❹ to ❼ return, 5 km.

♦ **Time from CBD:** 1 hour

♦ **Duration:** Short day

♦ **Children:** 9 years+

♦ **Nearest Refreshment:** Kurnell

♦ **Water:** Picnic area near start point. Carry water

♦ **Toilets:** Picnic area near start point.

♦ **Track:** Signposted; obvious; 5½ km unconstructed; some uneven surfaces; facilities; moderate–high use.

♦ **Ups 'n' downs:** Almost level.

♦ **Start:** Botany Bay National Park Visitor's Centre, off Polo St, Kurnell.

TRACK NOTES

A pamphlet about this walk and a map are available from the Visitors' Centre.

♦ From the Visitors' Centre, walk in a northerly direction across the picnic area to the water's edge. Proceed north-east (turn right), scrambling over the rocks around Sutherland Point. Do not attempt this when the seas are high.

♦ Follow the rocks for about 400 m and climb the steps ❶ to Cape Solander Dr. Follow the road south towards Cape Solander car park ❹. A detour at ❷ will take you to more rocks and the Yenna picnic area ❸. Don't miss the rock platform with cross-bedding and joints, and in the heath vegetation specimens of Coast Rosemary and Wax Flower.

♦ Once at the car park, take the track south along the cliff, across short stretches of heath to Tabbigai Gap ❺ and Blue Hole Gorge ❻, both of which are eroded dykes. *Take care near the cliff because there are no protective fences.* The heath features Flannel Flower, drumsticks, and dense mounds of Swamp She-oak near the cliff edge. Note the sand dunes and the dune scrub above the sandstone cliffs, and the swamps (or swales) in hollows among the dunes. Continue on to Cape Baily Lighthouse ❼ 🍎.

♦ The return trip can be varied by taking the Cape Baily Track from Tabbigai Gap or the Yena Track.

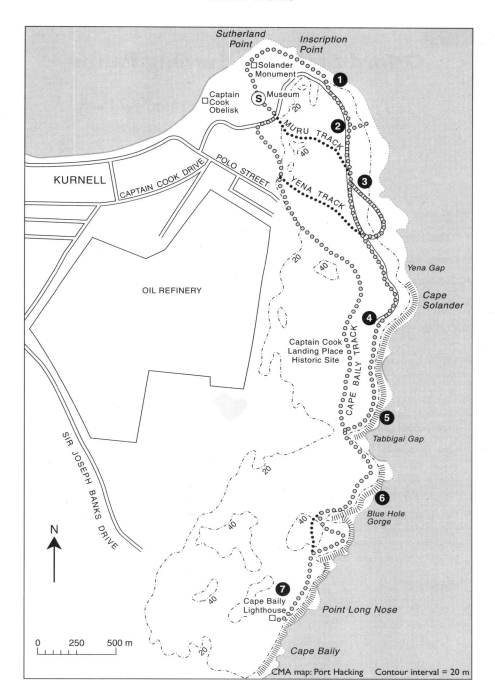

Sutherland
Point

Inscription
Point

Solander
Monument

1

Captain
Cook
Obelisk

Museum

S

20

MURU TRACK

2

40

YENA TRACK

3

KURNELL

CAPTAIN COOK DRIVE

POLO STREET

Yena Gap

Cape
Solander

20

40

OIL REFINERY

4

Captain Cook
Landing Place
Historic Site

CAPE BAILY TRACK

5

Tabbigai Gap

SIR JOSEPH BANKS DRIVE

20

6

Blue Hole
Gorge

40

40

N

7

Cape Baily
Lighthouse

Point Long Nose

40

0   250   500 m

20

Cape Baily

CMA map: Port Hacking   Contour interval = 20 m

No. 2

Otford Station – Burning Palms

This panoramic walk in the Royal National Park encompasses an area of distinctive rainforest, a delightful swimming beach, and clifftop views

- **Length:** 11 km

- **Time from CBD:** 1 hour; rail access

- **Duration:** Day

- **Children:** 9 years+

- **Nearest Refreshment:** Otford

- **Water:** Burning Palms; Otford Railway Station (might not be open). Carry water

- **Toilets:** Burning Palms; Otford Railway Station (might not be open)

- **Track:** Some signposting; 9 km unconstructed; obvious; some uneven surfaces; some facilities; moderate–high use

- **Ups 'n' downs:** One steep descent (110 in 350 m); one steep/moderate ascent (210 in 1800 m); several short moderate ascents and descents

- **Start:** (a) Car park at Otford Gap on Lady Wakehurst Dr, which can be accessed from Waterfall via McKell Ave; *or* (b) Otford Railway Station.

TRACK NOTES

◆ From the station, take the paved walkway on the eastern side of the railway line. After a short climb you will come to a dirt track which continues steeply up the ridge. Follow this track to a gravel road that goes directly to Wakehurst Dr (a shop is nearby). Walk north (left) for a few hundred metres to Otford Gap ❶. Here you will find samples of red claystone soil, and a south-easterly view of littoral rainforest above Bulgo Beach.

◆ The track from ❶ is signposted 'Werrong Beach (Hell Hole)'. Follow the track for 250 m uphill to a track fork ❷. Ignore the side-track that bypasses this fork. Enjoy here the view of the coastline and the Illawarra Escarpment; there is a marked contrast between the vertical sandstone cliffs on the top of the escarpment and the gentler, more shaly lower slopes.

◆ Take the left branch, signposted 'Coast Walk Burning Palms Track', and continue across the plateau to a second junction ❸. The right-hand track marked 'Palm Jungle Track' is the one you want. Follow it south-east to Werrong Point ❹ for more views of Greater Wollongong and Port Kembla. The vegetation above Hell Hole clearly shows the effects of salt-laden wind.

◆ Follow the track around Werrong Point, ignoring a faint track which goes off to the south (right). Continue on the

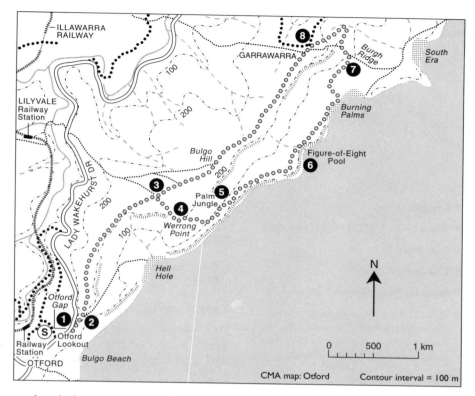

ILLAWARRA RAILWAY

GARRAWARRA

Burgh Ridge

South Era

LILYVALE Railway Station

Burning Palms

Bulgo Hill

Figure-of-Eight Pool

LADY WAKEHURST DR

Palm Jungle

Werrong Point

Hell Hole

N

Otford Gap

Otford Lookout

Railway Station

OTFORD

Bulgo Beach

0   500   1 km

CMA map: Otford   Contour interval = 100 m

track as it descends through Palm Jungle ❺, an impressive stand of littoral rainforest featuring Cabbage Tree Palm and Deciduous Fig, with its sculptured trunk and roots.

◆ Beyond Palm Jungle, the track crosses a stretch of grassland with a view of Burning Palms Beach. The track passes a ranger's hut and a sign indicating toilets before reaching the beach ●. There are thickets of Lilly-Pilly here — look for the edible pink fruit — and, time and tide permitting, take a 3-km round trip south along the wave-cut platform to the Figure-of-Eight Pool ❻.

◆ The exit track starts beside the Surf Life Saving Club's building, initially climbing north-west before swinging north-east to a track junction ❼ on Burgh Ridge. Turn left and proceed north on the main track, rather than taking the short, steep westerly short-cut, for an easier climb to Garrawarra car park ❽. Note the red claystone soil below the line of cliffs.

◆ From ❽, take the signposted Cliff Track (or fire trail), which heads generally south-west through medium/tall eucalypt forest featuring Blackbutt. Ignore tracks to the left and right. You will pass the track to Burning Palms used earlier in the day before reaching Otford Gap.

No. 3

Wodi–Wodi Track

This relatively demanding track at Stanwell Park features beach and panoramas, heath, and attractive forest vegetation

- **Length:** 6½ km
- **Time from CBD:** 1 hour; rail access
- **Duration:** Short day
- **Children:** 11 years+
- **Nearest Refreshment:** Stanwell Park
- **Water:** Adjacent to parking area at Stanwell Park Beach; Stanwell Park Railway Station (might be locked when station unattended). Carry water
- **Toilets:** As for water
- **Track:** Some signposting; 5½ km unconstructed; generally obvious; very uneven in places; some facilities; moderate use
- **Ups 'n' downs:** One steep/moderate ascent (100 in 600 m) and one very steep ascent (130 in 400 m); several shorter steep and moderate ascents and descents
- **Start:** Stanwell Park Railway Station. For car travellers, an alternative start (and finish) is the parking area at Stanwell Park Beach.

TRACK NOTES

Do not attempt the walk when the track is likely to be wet. Leaf litter makes part of the track slippery even in dry conditions.

◆ Follow the road from the station to the front of 'Hillcrest' ❶, formerly the home of the flight pioneer, Lawrence Hargrave. Take the pathway to the right and cross the bridge over the Lawrence Hargrave Dr. You can walk straight ahead along Station St to the beach or, for pleasant scenery, turn left along the Drive to the tennis courts and then follow the track to the beach picnic area.

◆ The track to the beach goes south from the end of Station St ❷. Follow the track past Stanwell Park Lagoon, noting the benched Narrabeen sandstones and shales in the southern headland, to the marked track from the beach to Kallaroo Ave.

Native Grape, *Cissus hypoglauca*

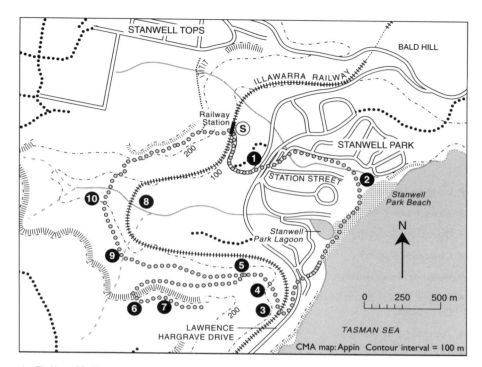

STANWELL TOPS

BALD HILL

ILLAWARRA RAILWAY

Railway
Station
S

STANWELL PARK

1

STATION STREET

2

10

8

Stanwell
Park Beach

N

9

Stanwell
Park Lagoon

5

4

6   **7**

3

0   250   500 m

LAWRENCE
HARGRAVE DRIVE

TASMAN SEA

CMA map: Appin Contour interval = 100 m

◆ Follow Kallaroo Ave up and round to its junction with Lower Coast Rd. The track to Lawrence Hargrave Dr is right at this junction, but the start could be obscure. At the Drive, there are two options, neither ideal. One is to turn south (left) and walk (*mindful of the traffic*) 250 m to the tunnel **3** under the railway. The other is to cross the Drive directly and take a track which is overgrown in places — ignore a side-track up to the railway lines.

◆ From the tunnel, cross the stile and follow the track up the grassy slope to the interpretation sign **4**. Continue on the now wide track (formerly a route used by the Wodi-Wodi people and later as a bullock track) through tall

Blackbutt forest to a track junction **5** indicated by the remnants of a sign.

◆ Take the track to the south (left) for a steep but rewarding climb through a medium eucalypt forest featuring Two-veined Hickory, and through a patch of heath dominated by Heath Banksia to the viewpoint **7** 👁. Enjoy excellent views of Stanwell Park, Bald Hill and the Sydney skyline, and the railway viaduct at **8**, the tallest in Australia.

◆ Return to the Wodi-Wodi Track and turn west (left). Follow the track across the creeks and through gully forest at **9** and **10** (there are markers in places). After climbing very steeply, the track levels out, passes the Stanwell Tops Track then drops to the railway station.

No. 4

Curra Moors Circuit

Heathland wildflowers and spectacular cliff and coastline views are showcased on this renowned Royal National Park circuit near Wattamolla

- **Length:** 10 km
- **Time from CBD:** 1 hour
- **Duration:** Short day
- **Children:** 9 years+
- **Nearest Refreshment:** Wattamolla
- **Water:** Audley; Garie Beach; Wattamolla. Carry water
- **Toilets:** As for water
- **Track:** Signposting; constructed (part fire trail); obvious; some eroded surfaces; no facilities; moderate–high use
- **Ups 'n' downs:** One moderate ascent (60 in 900 m); one moderate descent (60 in 900 m)

- **Start:** Parking area on Sir Bertram Stevens Dr, about 1 km north of the Garie Beach turn-off.

TRACK NOTES

♦ Take the Curra Moors Track north-east from the car park down through the woodland. The track levels and widens into a four-wheel-drive trail, which is followed in a north-easterly direction to the coast. Ignore the track going off to the south-east (right) at ❶ and the service road entering from the north (left) at ❷. The track passes through heath vegetation, and offers fine views of the coastline, the Illawarra Escarpment and Wollongong.

♦ At the junction of the Curra Moors and Coast tracks, turn north (left) and proceed to the Curracurrong Falls and Eagle Rock ❸. This is a splendid viewing and lunch spot ❺. *Take extreme care near the cliff edge because there is no safety fence.* Note the extensive marine cliff erosion and sweeping seascapes north and south.

♦ To return, follow the Coast Track south for about 2 km, leaving it at ❹ to take the track which goes off to the west (right). When the Curra Moors Track is rejoined at ❶, turn west (left) for the walk back up to the car park.

Sea cliffs in the Royal National Park

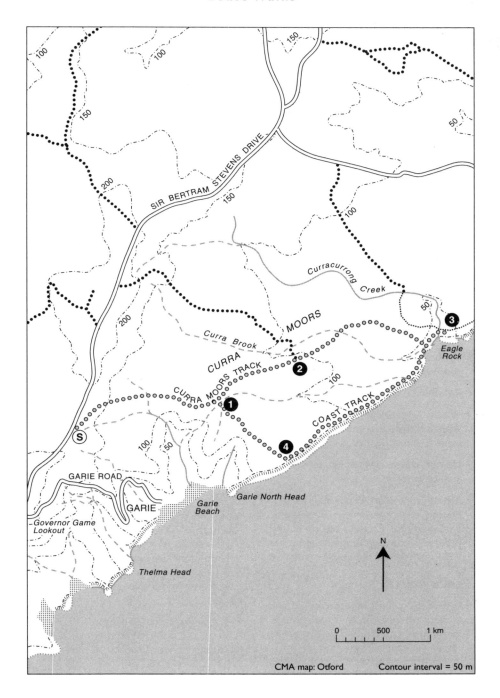

CMA map: Otford   Contour interval = 50 m

No. 5

Bundeena – Marley Head

Take this circuit through the Royal National Park to enjoy Aboriginal rock carvings, clifftop panoramas, and heath and dune vegetation

- **Length:** 13 km; or the track from ❸ back to Jibbon Beach (5½ km)

- **Time from CBD:** 1½ hours; rail (plus ferry) access

- **Duration:** Day

- **Children:** 11 years+

- **Nearest Refreshment:** Bundeena

- **Water:** Reserve on the corner of Loftus and Brighton Sts. Carry water

- **Toilets:** As for water

- **Track:** Signposting; 7½ km unconstructed; obvious; some uneven surfaces; some facilities; moderate–high use

- **Ups 'n' downs:** Two short, steep ascents and descents

- **Start:** Ferry wharf, Bundeena. The Bundeena ferry leaves the Gunnamatta Bay wharf near Cronulla Station on the half-hour, returning on the hour (tel. 02 9523 2990 for more details).

TRACK NOTES

◆ From the wharf, take the stone steps and the path east through the reserve to The Avenue and along The Lambeth Walk to the end of Neil St and the track to Jibbon Beach. Walk along the

beach and then for about 200 m around the rocks at the northern end to just before a small rock overhang ❶. Ignore all tracks to the right before this point. This part of the walk features coastal dune scrub, including Tuckeroo, She-oaks, Honey-reed and banksia species, as well as wave-cut platforms and evidence of jointing.

◆ Make the short climb to the top of the rocks. Follow the track along the edge, around the top of a small gully and then on to a T-junction. Turn north (left). About 100 m from the junction, the track returns to the cliff edge for a short distance (ignore the rough track going off to the east), before swinging east and south up onto a large rock platform ❷. Look for Aboriginal (Dharawal people) engravings on the rock.

◆ At the Y-junction, just beyond the southern end of the rock platform, turn north-east (left) and follow the track to a T-junction. Go east (left) up the ridge and then south through heath to a grassy area overlooking a small beach ❸ 🍎.

◆ From the beach, turn south. Ignore the track to the west (right) which goes to Jibbon Beach. Proceed to a small grassy clearing and junction at ❹ and

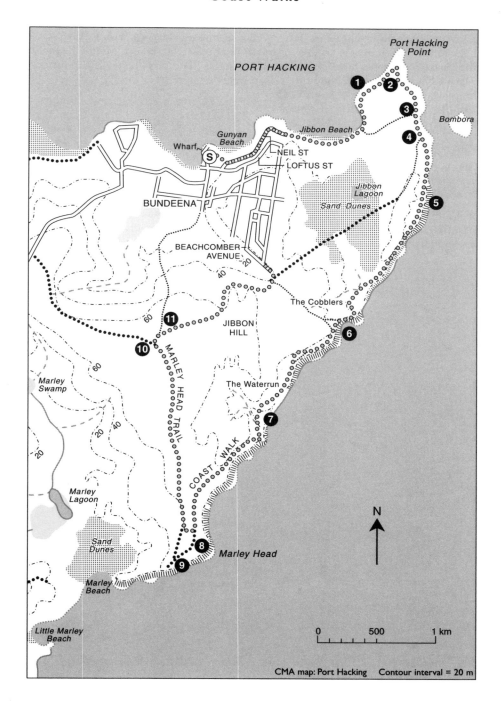

PORT HACKING

Port Hacking Point

Bombora

Jibbon Beach

Gunyan Beach

Wharf

NEIL ST

LOFTUS ST

Jibbon Lagoon

Sand Dunes

BUNDEENA

BEACHCOMBER AVENUE

The Cobblers

JIBBON HILL

The Waterrun

MARLEY HEAD TRAIL

Marley Swamp

Marley Lagoon

COAST WALK

Sand Dunes

Marley Head

Marley Beach

Little Marley Beach

N

0   500   1 km

CMA map: Port Hacking   Contour interval = 20 m

take the lesser track south-east (left) back to the cliff line. Stay on this track, the Coast Walk, to its junction with the Marley Head Trail at **9**. Note the remains of the military lookouts at **5** and **6**. The heath features Crimson Bottlebrush, Tick Bush and Pigface. Also keep an eye out for lizards (skinks), and for jointing in the rock. Across some of the rocky cliff tops, the track is not obvious, but its location is generally within 20 to 30 m of the edge.

◆ From the Waterrun crossing at **7**, go east (left) across the rock platform and *not* straight up the slope. Take time to visit Marley Head **8**, with its fine views of Marley Beach, Marley Lagoon and the coastline. There are also rock engravings here.

◆ At **9**, turn north (right) and follow the Marley Head Trail to the track junction at **10**, which is located about 100 m beyond where the Marley Head Trail swings west (left). At the junction, turn north (right). At the intersection **11** about 150 m from the junction, ignore the left- and right-hand options, but go straight ahead. Soon the track swings east (right), eventually linking with Beachcomber Ave, Bundeena.

Wave-cut platform, Royal National Park

Maitland Bay Centre – Putty Beach

Enjoy ocean views and diverse vegetation and landforms on this very attractive walk in Bouddi National Park north of Killcare

- **Length:** 6 km; or from ❶ to ❸, 2 km.
- **Time from CBD:** 2 hours
- **Duration:** Half day
- **Children:** 9 years+
- **Nearest Refreshment:** Killcare
- **Water:** Putty Beach camping area. Carry water
- **Toilets:** As for water
- **Track:** Some signposting; mainly natural but constructed steps and stretch of boardwalk; obvious; some uneven surfaces; some facilities; moderate–high use
- **Ups 'n' downs:** One moderate to steep descent (100 in 800 m); one moderate ascent (140 in 1000 m)
- **Start:** Maitland Bay Visitor's Centre, near the intersection of The Scenic Rd and Maitland Bay Dr.

TRACK NOTES

◆ From the car park behind the Centre ❶, follow the Maitland Bay Track for about 150 m before turning south (right) at ❷ to take the Bullimah Spur Track to Bullimah Lookout ❸ for a view of Putty Beach, Box Head

Peninsula, Barrenjoey Head and Lion Island (south-west).

◆ Return to the Maitland Bay Track at ❷, turn east (right) and proceed for several hundred metres to where a rough track off to the left (just before a flight of stone stairs) takes you to a rock outcrop ❹, with views of Maitland Bay, Bouddi Point and Maitland Bombora (south-east).

◆ Rejoin the main track and proceed down to its junction with the Putty Beach Track ❺. The medium eucalypt forest here includes Smooth-barked Apple, Blackbutt, Red Bloodwood, as well as casuarina and banksia species. There is also abundant birdlife in the area, including Brush Turkey.

◆ A very worthwhile option is to devote 40 to 60 minutes to make a return trip (2 km) to Bouddi Point 🍎 to view the richly patterned cliff face, rock platform and wreck of the *S.S. Maitland* (foundered in 1898 with the loss of 24 lives). Otherwise, turn south-west (right) and make your way to Gerrin Point ❻, with its view of Barrenjoey Headland and the coastline north of Sydney (south-west). The vegetation here is low eucalypt forest, including the unusual Dwarf Plum-pine conifer,

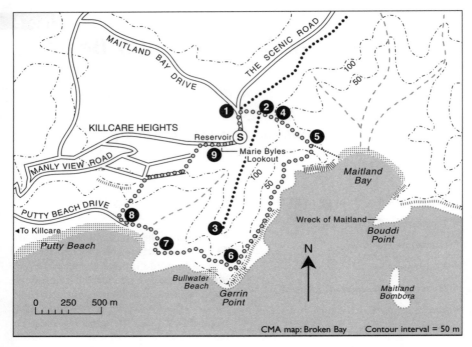

Burrawang, Grass-tree, Smooth-barked apple and Coast Rosemary.

♦ Continue on to the headland above the eastern end of Putty Beach ❼, and note the wave-cut platform and tessellated pavement, the patterned sandstone on the cliff edge, and the rust-coloured joints.

♦ Proceed to the beach ❻ and the road that goes behind the vegetated dunes to the NPWS Camping Area ❽. A track at the back right-hand corner of the first camping bay takes you up to McDonald St. Turn east (right) and continue to the turning circle at the end and onto the track up to The Scenic Road. Turn east (right) and, after a pause at the Marie Byles Lookout ❾ to view the entrance to Broken Bay, Manly, and Centrepoint Tower, return to the start.

Take great care on The Scenic Road as there is no footpath.

Coast Rosemary, *Westringia fruticosa*

Frazer Beach – Moonee Beach

Swim, walk through heath and dune vegetation, and explore fascinating geological feaures such as sea caves in Munmorah State Recreation Area

- **Length:** 8 km; or return from Timber Beach, 4 km
- **Time from CBD**: 2 hours
- **Duration:** Short day
- **Children:** 9 years+
- **Nearest Refreshment:** Lake Munmorah
- **Water:** Frazer Beach car park. Carry water
- **Toilets:** As for water
- **Track:** Limited signposting; 3 km unconstructed; obvious; some uneven surfaces; some facilities; moderate–high use
- **Ups 'n' downs:** Two steep descents (80 in 500 m; 60 in 300 m); one steep (80 in 500 m) and two moderate (50 in 800 m, 90 in 900 m) ascents
- **Start:** Frazer Beach car park, Munmorah SRA, the entrance to which is east of the Pacific Hwy, just north of Lake Munmorah. Within the SRA, the road route to Frazer Beach is signposted.

TRACK NOTES

(a) *Parts of the track are very slippery when wet.* (b) *Time the walk to coincide with a very low (0.2 m or less) tide.* (c) *Take a torch, swimmers and light footwear for wading.*

◆ Take the stairs to the beach, walk north-east (left) and then proceed up across the headland to Bongon Beach and on to the memorial cairn at the end of Snapper Point, where the Snapper Head conglomerate is obvious. An eroded north-south joint ❶ is visible from beyond the fence. *Exercise great care approaching and viewing it.*

◆ Return to Snapper Point car park and the viewing point for Frazer Blowhole ❷ (not active at low tide). Take the road from the car park to the fence at the first curve ❸. Proceed (carefully) to the rock platform just beyond the fence. Note the natural arch above the entrance on the north side of Frazer Inlet ❹.

◆ Continue up the road, via the lookout at ❺, to the road junction at ❻. Turn east (right) and go on to the second lookout ❼ and then down the track through heathland to Timber Beach, where there are sedimentary layers in the surrounding rocks ⑥.

◆ *Tide and waves permitting*, locate one of several obvious entrances ❽ to the cavern behind the cliffs just south of

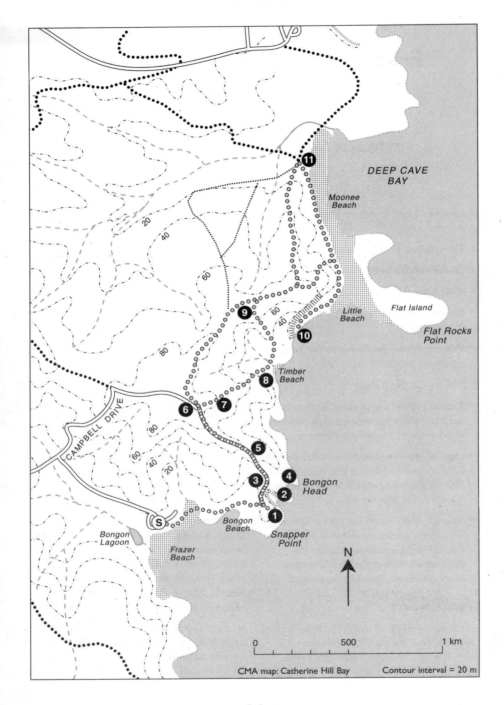

DEEP CAVE
BAY

Moonee
Beach

Flat Island

Little
Beach

Flat Rocks
Point

Timber
Beach

CAMPBELL DRIVE

Bongon
Head

Bongon
Lagoon

Bongon Beach

Snapper
Point

Frazer
Beach

N

0   500   1 km

CMA map: Catherine Hill Bay   Contour interval = 20 m

the beach. Explore the cavern, being prepared for some wading, rough surfaces underfoot, and semi-darkness.

♦ From Timber Beach, take the track north (right) up the spur to a Y-junction ❾. The right-hand option (slightly overhung with vegetation) joins the Moonee Beach Trail. Follow the trail east (right) for about 200 m to where a narrow track goes off to the right. Take this track (eroded in places) to Moonee Beach. Once at the beach, turn south and walk to the southern end of Little Beach.Observe the Permian sedimen-tary strata (conglomerate/coal seam/conglomerate) in the cliff here; note the spit (tombala) out to Flat Island, and explore the cave (negotiable) at ❿.

♦ Retrace your steps to Moonee Beach, linking up with a constructed track at ⓫. Follow this track for about 200 m, turning sharply west (left) onto a wide trail which is followed for about 100 m to the Moonee Beach Trail. Take the Moonee Beach Trail up and along the ridge to Snapper Point Rd. Make your way east (left) back to Snapper Point and then across to Frazer Beach.

Christmas Bells, *Blandfordia nobilis*

Walks on the Hornsby Plateau (North)

The first five of the Hornsby Plateau walks provide delightful views of the inlets of Broken Bay. All but walk 14 pass through forests and heaths typical of Hawkesbury Sandstone country. The walks are especially attractive, therefore, during the wildflower season — late winter and spring. The majestic forests encountered on walk 14 make it an attractive proposition almost any time. Sandstone caves are passed on several of the walks, but the cave visited on walk 12 is very special.

The Sphinx – Bobbin Head

Close to Sydney's sparkling northern beaches, this track in Ku-ring-gai Chase National Park features Aboriginal rock carvings and mixed vegetation

- **Length:** 9 km; or finish at Bobbin Head, 5 km
- **Time from CBD:** 45 minutes; train to Turramurra plus a Shorelink bus
- **Duration:** Short day
- **Children:** 9 years+
- **Nearest Refreshment:** Bobbin Head
- **Water:** Bobbin Head. Carry water
- **Toilets:** As for water
- **Track:** Some signposting; 5½ km unconstructed; obvious; sandy in places, some steps; some facilities; moderate–high use
- **Ups 'n' downs:** One moderate/steep descent (140 in 1500 m); one steep/moderate ascent (150 in 1400 m)
- **Start:** The entrance to Ku-ring-gai Chase National Park, Bobbin Head Rd, North Turramurra, or the Sphinx Memorial.

TRACK NOTES

♦ From the Park gates ❶, turn east (right) onto the sealed road leading to the Sphinx Memorial ❷. On the northwest side of the memorial there is a sealed track which ends after a few metres at a fire trail. Turn right onto the trail and then immediately left to join the track signposted Sphinx Track.

♦ The track descends steadily and steeply, crosses a creek and then descends again before reaching the junction ❸ with the Warrimoo Track. From here the track winds generally northwards along the banks of Cowan Water through a variety of vegetation, including medium eucalypt forest, Native Fuchsia, Boronia, Grass-tree and Heath Banksia. Note also the mangroves, saltmarsh, weathering of the sandstone cliffs and boulders, and the shell midden at ❹.

♦ As you reach the first moored boats at picturesque Bobbin Head, note the Bobbin Head Track going off to the south (left) ❺. This is the return route, but before heading off along it, spend time enjoying the facilities here at Bobbin Head 🍎.

♦ The walk up the Bobbin Head Track is steep at first but soon becomes an old road (the original Bobbin Head Rd instigated by Du Faur in 1890 and closed to vehicles in 1930), which zigzags more gently up the hill. Here the vegetation changes from medium to low eucalypt forest, and heath, with

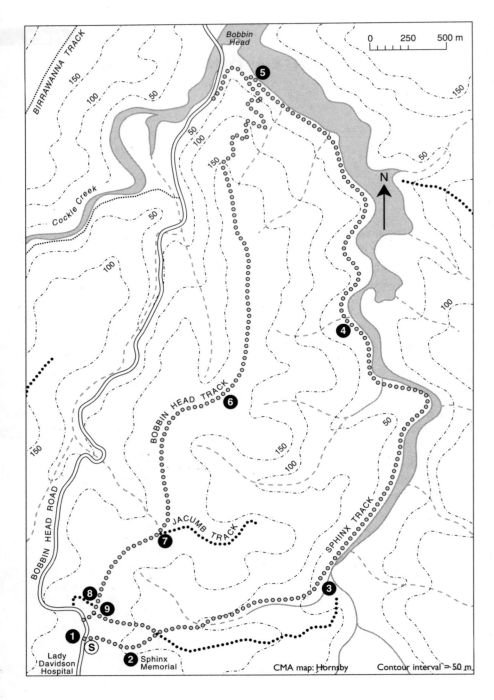

BIRRAWANNA TRACK

Bobbin
Head

5

150

100

50

Cockle Creek

50

100

150

50

100

N

150

100

4

50

BOBBIN HEAD TRACK

150

6

100

50

150

JACUMB TRACK

100

7

SPHINX TRACK

BOBBIN HEAD ROAD

150

8

3

9

1

S

2 Sphinx
Memorial

Lady
Davidson
Hospital

0   250   500 m

CMA map: Hornsby   Contour interval = 50 m.

grevilleas, Pink Wax Flower, and Dwarf Apple.

♦ About 500 m beyond where the track reaches the top of the ridge, look for, and enter a noticeable opening and clearing on the western (right-hand) side of the track ❻ to see Aboriginal rock carvings of a wallaby, goanna and other figures.

♦ The track continues generally south. Beyond the power lines, ignore Jacumb Track going off to the east (left) ❼ and, farther on, a track going off to the west (right) ❽. Just past this point, the Sphinx Track branches off to the east (left), but to return directly to the Park entrance, go on the few metres to the main road and then turn south (left).

Knob-sedge, *Isolepis nodosa*

No. 9

Mount Ku-ring-gai Station – Berowra Station via Berowra Creek

Encompassing a section of the Benowie Walking Track,
this route includes relaxing water views,
mangroves, and diverse forest types

◆ **Length:** 8½ km

◆ **Time from CBD:** 1 hour; rail access

◆ **Duration:** Short day

◆ **Children:** 9 years+

◆ **Nearest Refreshment:** Mount Ku-ring-gai, Berowra

◆ **Water:** Carry water

◆ **Toilets:** Mount Ku-ring-gai Railway Station (might be closed), at Berowra, behind the community hall

◆ **Track:** Some signposting; 1½ km constructed; generally obvious; some uneven surfaces, steps and a couple of short scrambles over rock; no facilities; light–moderate use

◆ **Ups 'n' downs:** One moderate descent (120 in 1000 m); one steep ascent (170 in 600 m)

◆ **Start:** Mount Ku-ring-gai Railway Station ❶.

TRACK NOTES

◆ From the station, Great North Walk (GNW) signs indicate the route — 400 m south along the Pacific Hwy to a footbridge and then back up the

highway for about 30 m to Glenview Ave to the start of the Benowie Track (which joins the GNW).

◆ For the first 500 m, the track is on sealed road and then fire trail. Follow it to a clearing where several fire trails meet ❷. Take the extreme left-hand option, which is signposted to indicate the GNW. After crossing a drainage line, the track narrows and follows Lyrebird Gully through medium eucalypt forest featuring Smooth-barked Apple. Markers in the form of red triangles are placed at intervals.

◆ About 1 km farther on, the track crosses the creek, eventually occupying the rocky creek bed and becoming a little indistinct. Here there is a sharp change from 'dry' to 'moist' vegetation, with the shrub *Astrotricha floccosa* in abundance (note the minute star-shaped hairs covering its leaves).

◆ The track continues on the eastern (right-hand) side of the creek, climbing above it. Two overhangs ❸ and ❹ are passed. About 200 m beyond the second, the track turns sharply west (left) at a tree marked with a red tape and descends again to the creek. After following the creek on the eastern

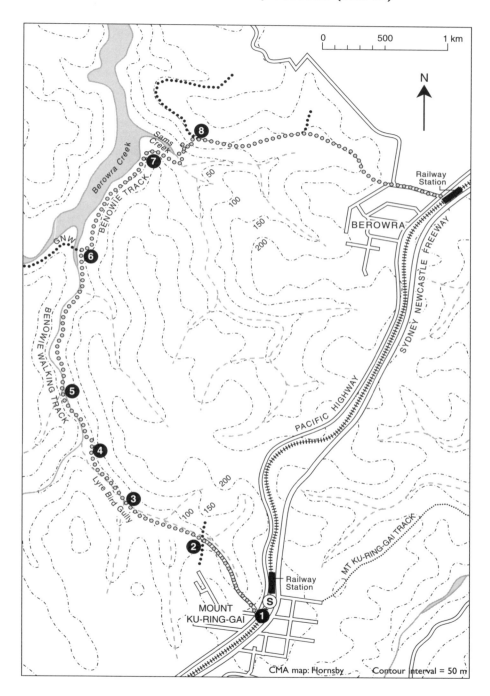

0   500   1 km

N

Railway Station

BEROWRA

SYDNEY NEWCASTLE FREEWAY

Berowra Creek

Sams Creek

BENOWIE TRACK

GNW

BENOWIE WALKING TRACK

PACIFIC HIGHWAY

Lyre Bird Gully

MT KU-RING-GAI TRACK

Railway Station

MOUNT KU-RING-GAI

CMA map: Hornsby   Contour interval = 50 m

(right-hand) side for 150 m, the track crosses the creek (look for the red triangle markers). In about 200 m, a large rock pool ❺ is passed and the track re-crosses the creek.

◆ From here the track follows the western (right-hand) side of the creek to the junction with the GNW ❻. Note the mangrove trees here, and their pneumatophores, which aerate the roots, protruding from the mud).

◆ From the junction, the track continues east on a boardwalk across a salt-marsh area featuring Samphire and

Knob-sedge, and along the mangrove-fringed Berowra Creek, an arm of a drowned river valley or ria, to a rock outcrop ❼ 🍎 above Sams Creek.

◆ The track then descends steeply to Sams Creek and follows it upstream, and after crossing it ascends steeply to a junction with a fire trail ❽. At the junction, turn east (right) and follow the fire trail until it swings north to Joalah Creek. Leave the trail here and proceed east on the obvious track (ignore all side-branches) and up the short, steep climb to Crowley Rd and street access to Berowra Station.

Jerusalem Bay

Cowan Station – Hawkesbury River Station

Enjoy this scenically diverse river track meandering through Ku-ring-gai Chase National Park to the Hawkesbury River at Brooklyn

◆ **Length:** 11 km

◆ **Time from CBD:** 1 hour; rail access

◆ **Duration:** Day

◆ **Children:** 11 years+

◆ **Nearest Refreshment:** Brooklyn

◆ **Water:** Cowan and Hawkesbury River stations. Carry water

◆ **Toilets:** As for water

◆ **Track:** Signposting; 6 km unconstructed; obvious; many uneven surfaces; no facilities; light–moderate use

◆ **Ups 'n' downs:** Two moderate (50 in 2000 m, 120 in 900 m) and one steep (100 in 500 m) descent and two steep ascents (190 in 500 m, 120 in 400 m)

◆ **Start:** Cowan Railway Station

TRACK NOTES

◆ From the steps on the eastern platform of Cowan Railway Station, follow the Great North Walk (GNW) signs north (left) for about 75 m and then turn east (right) at the sign-board. Cross the F3 Freeway on the pedestrian bridge. The track, passing through gully forest and past patches of Water Gum, then descends for about 2 km down Yarala Creek to an open area overlooking Jerusalem Bay ❶, an arm of a drowned river valley, with mangrove vegetation along the foreshores. Watch out for water birds and soldier crabs.

◆ The track follows the northern side of the creek and then climbs north-east up Govett Ridge. Campbells Crater not far west of the track is a valley diatreme. Note the tessellated pavement at ❷. After dropping to Campbells Creek, the track climbs again through medium eucalypt forest featuring Smooth-barked Apple to the ridge top. The (Hawkesbury) sandstone cave ❸, with iron staining and banding in the rocks, is a good spot to rest.

◆ On the ridge the track becomes a fire trail. A detour to the left near a sign indicating 'Brooklyn 6 km' provides a view of the F3 and the northern railway line ❹. *Take great care, as there is no fence.* There are clearly visible bedding planes in the (Hawkesbury) sandstone walls of the cutting.

◆ The walk now follows the fire trail in a northerly direction for about 2 km before turning east at a point offering a

View of the Hawkesbury River from Walk 10

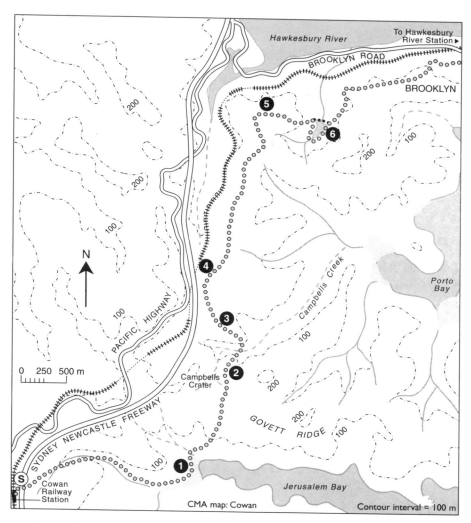

good view **5** of the road and rail bridges, and of the drowned Hawkesbury River valley **6**. Follow the rock ledge west for the best view.

◆ About 500 m east of **5**, a deviation from the direct route loops round Brooklyn Dam, a railway dam built to supply water for steam locomotives **6**.

A swim in the dam, pretty with non-native water lilies, is an option in warmer weather.

◆ Follow the fire trail north-east, ignoring the branches on both sides. A GNW sign indicates the track and steps that lead to Brooklyn Rd. It is only a short walk to shops and the railway station.

No. 11

Point Clare Station – Koolewong Ridge – Woy Woy Station

Discover remnants of ancient Aboriginal culture in the readily accessible Brisbane Water National Park

◆ **Length:** 10 km; or lunch at ❼ and omit ❽, 9km.

◆ **Time from CBD**: 1½ hours; rail access

◆ **Duration:** Short day

◆ **Children:** 9 years+

◆ **Nearest Refreshment:** Woy Woy

◆ **Water:** Carry water

◆ **Toilets:** Point Clare and Woy Woy Stations

◆ **Track:** Some signposting; 3 km unconstructed; generally obvious; some uneven surfaces; no facilities; light–moderate use

◆ **Ups 'n' downs:** Three moderate ascents; one moderate to steep descent (130 in 800 m)

◆ **Start:** From Point Clare Station, turn north (right) along Brisbane Water Dr. Take Penang St, the fourth on the left. The track starts at the top of Penang St. As the walk finishes at Woy Woy, cars can be left there and the train taken to Point Clare.

TRACK NOTES

◆ From the top of Penang St, follow the curling, well-defined track to its intersection with a fire trail ❶ for views of Gosford and Brisbane Water, a drowned river valley.

◆ Turn west (right) and follow the road to a four-way intersection ❷. Turn south (left) and make the steady descent to a small creek ❸ (might be dry). Downstream of ❸ are a waterfall, rock pools and an area of gully forest.

◆ Proceed up the road, past the gate into the National Park and on to the junction with Bambara Rd ❹. About 100 m from this junction, take the track branching off to the left ❺ past several boulders. Nearby is a rock platform ❻, with pleasant views across the bay and a less-than-obvious Aboriginal carving of a fish.

◆ Continue south-east through low eucalypt forest until you reach a 4 m-wide rock shaped like an anvil ❼ 🍎. The track is slightly overgrown, but its general direction is indicated in places by small metal markers on trees.

◆ Look for two direction marks (arrow heads — one up, one to the right here) on a nearby tree. Turn south-west (left) and walk 30 m through the bush to the fire trail. Cross the trail and continue on

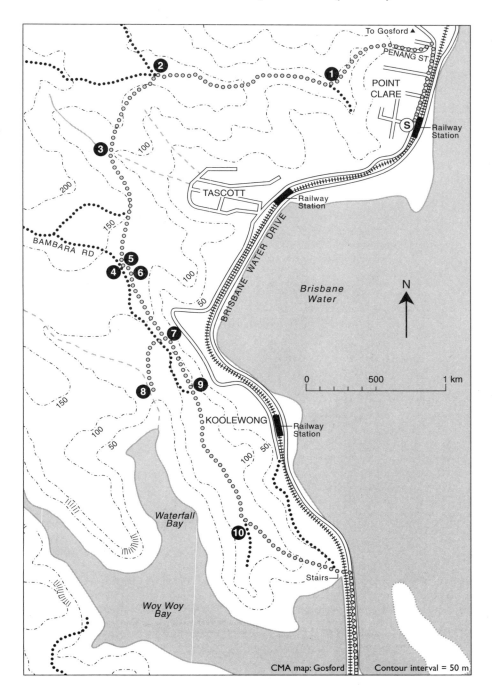

down the track to a creek (with pot-holes). Stay with the path on the left of the creek until you come to a rock plat-form ❽ with carvings of two men and a wallaby.

◆ Return to 'anvil' rock ❼ and turn south-east (right) along the cliff-top track. The track through medium eucalypt forest is obscure but goes to the left of some rocky outcrops and finally joins the fire trail at ❾. Look for the shell middens in a cave in the sandstone cliffs.

◆ Turn left at the fire trail, which is followed for 1¼ km to the second Y-intersection ❿. Turn left past the water tank to join a steep, badly eroded track (*take care here, especially after rain*). At the end of this track, ignore the road on the left to Koolewong Station. Walk down the concrete steps and under the railway line, then turn right onto Brisbane Water Dr and follow for 1 km to Woy Woy Station.

Native Hops, *Dodonaea triquetra*

Wondabyne Station – Pindar Cave

*Pindar Cave—a spectacular sandstone overhang—
spring wildflowers, and water views make this
Brisbane Water National Park walk
an absolute delight*

- **Length:** 12 km

- **Time from CBD:** 1-1½ hours; rail access only

- **Duration:** Day

- **Children:** 11 years+

- **Nearest Refreshment:** Wherever you join the train

- **Water:** Carry water

- **Toilets:** None

- **Track:** No signposting; 9 km unconstructed; generally obvious; some uneven surfaces and steps; no facilities; light use

- **Ups 'n' downs:** One steep ascent and descent (80 in 400 m); several short, moderate ascents and descents

- **Start:** Wondabyne rail platform. *Tell the train guard that you want to be let off at Wondabyne. Travel in the last carriage.*

TRACK NOTES

The walk is not suitable in hot weather.

- The track starts from the Sydney end of the platform, goes south for a short distance and then climbs steeply to the top of the ridge ❶, where the track becomes a fire trail. Enjoy views of Mullet Creek and the quarry from the ridge, and note the stand of Forest She-oaks on the side of the ridge.

- Follow the trail for about 1 km to a track junction ❷. Take the fire trail which goes off to the west (left). After 400 m, the fire trail becomes a track. Note how run-off from the nearby rocks supports a moist heath habitat. The mix of heath and low eucalypt forest, here and elsewhere in the walk is also of interest.

- Follow the track to a saddle, Lysippus Pass. The short descent from the second rock outcrop that is crossed is slightly to the right and not straight ahead. Where the track divides before the saddle, take the left-hand option. Proceed across Timotheus Heights to the rock platforms at ❸ (Lysippus, Timotheus and Pindar—ancient Greek sculptor and poets, respectively). The second rock platform is surfaced by a tessellated pavement created by joints.

- From ❸ the track crosses another saddle and then climbs to the Timotheus Causeway. A rock outcrop on the left near the top of the climb ❹ provides a view of Mooney Mooney Creek. The track continues south

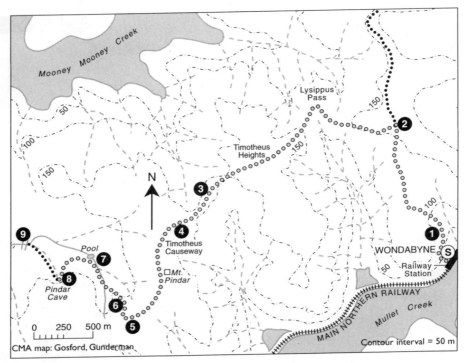

CMA map: Gosford, Gunderman

Contour interval = 50 m

across Mount Pindar to rock outcrops and a point **5** providing views of Broken Bay, a drowned river valley; Dangar Island; and, on the horizon, the Baha'i Temple at Ingleside.

◆ From **5** the track drops steadily and then more steeply to a watercourse, finally reaching a waterhole **7**. At a rock outcrop **6**, the track goes right for about 5 m, not directly ahead. Pindar Cave **8**, formerly used by Aborigines, is 400 m beyond **7** 🍎.

Features of the cave include 'iron stone' colouring and banding, the inter-bedding of sandstone and softer rocks, and the honeycomb weathering and deposits of salt crystals inside some of the deeper cavities. The track from **8** to the waterfall **9** is a delightful optional extension.

◆ Return by the same route, keeping left where the track divides on Timotheus Heights.

Mill Creek Circuit

*Pristine creeks, wildflowers and a variety of forest types
are showcased on this relatively demanding walk in
Dharug National Park near Wisemans Ferry*

◆ **Length:** 11 km

◆ **Time from CBD:** 1½ hours

◆ **Duration:** Long day

◆ **Children:** 11 years+

◆ **Nearest Refreshment:** Wisemans
Ferry

◆ **Water:** Water at camping area on right-
hand branch of access road to Mill Creek
picnic area. Carry water

◆ **Toilets:** Mill Creek picnic area

◆ **Track:** Some signposting; 9 km unconstructed; uneven and narrow in parts;
obvious; some facilities; low usage

◆ **Ups 'n' downs:** One moderate (80 in
2000 m) and three steep (100 in 600 m,
80 in 600 m, 100 in 1000 m) ascents, and
three steep/moderate (90 in 500 m, 90 in
400 m, 180 in 2000 m) descents

◆ **Start:** At the south-east corner of the
Mill Creek picnic area. At Wisemans
Ferry, cross the river and turn right.
After about 5 km, take the signposted
road left to the picnic area and entrance
to Dharug National Park. Both ends of
the track are signposted.

*You can start the walk from the north-east
corner of the picnic area and head in the
reverse direction.*

TRACK NOTES

◆ Just beyond the start ❶, the track
branches. Take the left-hand branch
that follows the creek for a distance and
then climbs away from the creek on the
south side. Where the track returns to
the creek, there is a burnt-out bridge
❷. The alternative crossing is not
obvious, and mossy boulders make it
slippery. This part of the walk features
a lovely stand of tall eucalypt forest,
with Sydney Blue Gum, Rough-barked
Apple, Coachwood and Grey Myrtle
along the creek.

◆ The track climbs the side of the
valley, goes round two gullies and then
returns to the valley floor ❸. From
here it goes north-east (left). Ignore the
track that goes straight ahead to
nowhere. Here the forest is medium
eucalypt, including Smooth-barked
Apple, Turpentine, Forest She-oak and
Forest Grass-tree.

◆ Follow the track as it makes its way
up a steep gully and through the cliff
line to a level rocky saddle ❹. The
gully forest features turpentine trees,
and a tall understorey with Graceful
Bush-pea and Gymea Lily. At the
saddle, there is a sudden change of
vegetation to low eucalypt forest, with

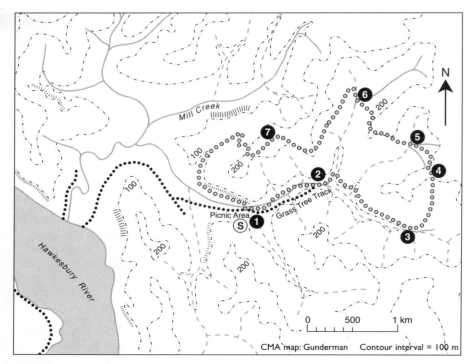

plenty of Yellow Bloodwood, Narrow-leaved Apple and Wax flower.

◆ From the saddle, the track veers slightly to the north (right) and drops into a valley down to a small creek ❺ 🍎. The flora changes from dry euca-lypt forest to a taller forest on the sandy valley floor.

◆ Follow the track up and around a spur to another valley and creek ❻. Note the rock bar and potholes in the creek bed.

◆ A longish but not very steep climb follows as the track goes south-west around another spur, past a huge fallen slab of (Hawkesbury) sandstone and onto the saddle at ❼. Look out for the large Blue-leaved Stringybark trees near the top of the spur. There is yet another change to drier, sparser forest at the saddle, with Yellow Bloodwood dominating.

◆ From the saddle, the track continues west until it turns north (right) and descends steeply to another valley. Before entering a narrow ravine at the beginning of the final descent, the track skirts around large outcrops of bare rock.

◆ Below the cliff line, the track sidles across the hillside before dropping to a wooden bridge providing access to the picnic area and its tall eucalypt forest. Watch out for wombats and wallabies here at dusk.

No. 14

Pines Forest Picnic Area – Abbotts Falls

Discover a pleasant waterfall and patches of rainforest on this lovely walk in Watagan State Forest west of Morriset and Cooranbong

◆ **Length:** 8 km; or several other options

◆ **Time from CBD**: 2½ hours

◆ **Duration:** Short day

◆ **Children:** 9 years+

◆ **Nearest Refreshment:** Cooranbong

◆ **Water:** Pines Forest Park and nearby picnic areas. Carry water

◆ **Toilets:** As for water

◆ **Track:** Signposting; unconstructed with some development (3 km); obvious; mainly even surface but slippery when wet; facilities; low–moderate use

◆ **Ups 'n' downs:** One moderate to steep descent (130 in 700 m); one moderate to steep ascent (110 in 1300 m)

◆ **Start:** Pines Forest picnic area ❶. Exit F3 to Morisset and at the second roundabout turn left into Freemans Dr. After about 6½ km, turn left into Martinsville Rd (note the 'Watagan Forest' sign). Turn left into Martinsville Hill Rd at the next 'Watagan Forest' sign after 4½ km. Follow this road, taking care to veer right where it joins the Watagan Forest Rd. A sign will indicate the right-hand turn into Palmers Rd and the Pines picnic area. Note the sixty-year-old plantation of Slash Pines at ❶.

TRACK NOTES

Attempt this walk only when the track is dry.

◆ From the Palmers Rd entrance to the picnic area, follow the road east (left) for 200 m and then take the clearly signposted track veering off to the right. Green ↑ signs make the track easy to follow. At Abbotts Rd, the sign indicates a left-turn up the road to where another sign indicates the track to Dora Creek going off to the south-east (right).

◆ Follow the track through medium eucalypt forest into the valley. Beyond where it crosses a side-creek ❷, the track may be obscured by leaf litter for a short distance. Here, continue east (straight ahead) parallel to the side-creek. The Dora Creek crossing and Abbotts Falls ❸ are a short distance farther on ◆. There are lovely patches of rainforest here, featuring Bangalow Palm; and note the Elkhorn fern in the tree to the left of the crossing ❸.

◆ Just past the crossing, look for the earth-filled platform ❹ from where you can see Bird's-nest ferns and an obscured view of the falls. From here the track rises steeply in places to

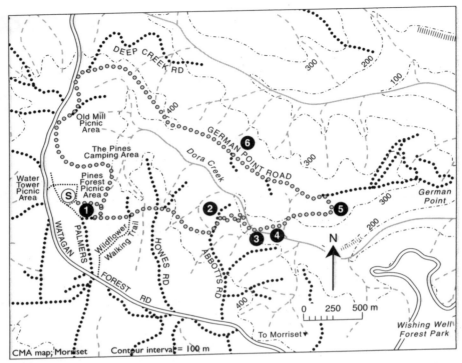

German Point Rd. This is a tall eucalypt forest area, with its typical species
of Turpentine, Round-leaved Blue
Gum, Sydney Blue Gum, stringybarks,
Spotted Gum and Blackbutt. Spot the
orchid in a large eucalypt at ➎.

◆ At German Point Rd, proceed west
(left). Just before the junction with
Watagan Forest Rd, a sign on the left
indicates a track to the Pines Picnic
Area. There is a pleasant view of Lake
Macquarie from ➏.

◆ Follow this track for about 100 m,
turning south (right) to go through the
Casuarina camping area and to the road
to Turpentine camping area. Take this
road to the far side of the camping area,
where a sign indicates the track across

and along a creek to the Pines camping
and picnic areas.

Lilly-pilly, Acmena smithii

Walks on the Woronora Plateau (South)

The first three walks in this group (15, 16 and 17) are in the Royal National Park, one of the first National Parks to be established anywhere in the world. The delights of these walks include forests and heathland as well as charming creeks, pools and waterfalls. Walk 17 passes through both tall eucalypt forest and rainforest. Walk 18 offers similar attractions to walks 15 and 16. All of these walks have particular appeal during the wildflower season — late spring to summer.

No. 15

Heathcote Station – Karloo Pool – Waterfall Station

Enjoy a delightful pool, a waterfall, forest and heath vegetation on this Royal National Park walk

- **Length:** 12 km; or return from ❶ to ❷, 6 km
- **Time from CBD**: 1 hour; rail access
- **Duration:** Day
- **Children:** 9 years+
- **Nearest Refreshment:** Heathcote
- **Water:** Carry water
- **Toilets:** Waterfall and Heathcote Stations (could be locked when station unattended)
- **Track:** Some signposting; 9 km unconstructed; obvious; uneven in places; no facilities; moderate–high use
- **Ups 'n' downs:** One moderate ascent (90 in 1000 m); one moderate descent (130 in 1500 m)
- **Start:** Eastern side of Heathcote Railway Station (park at either Heathcote or Waterfall Station).

TRACK NOTES

◆ Walk down the southern (right-hand) side of the Emergency Services compound and along the fire trail to the east. The Karloo Pool Track is on the right about 350 m from the start ❶.

Take this track to Karloo Pool ❷, which is surrounded by medium eucalypt forest dominated by Smooth-barked Apple.

◆ Cross the creek to the south side and take the track up and across the ridge to Uloola Falls, ❹ 🍎 pausing at Uloola Turrets ❸ for a view of the park and the Sydney skyline.

◆ From the Falls, follow the path up Uloola Brook *or*, for easier walking, take the old four-wheel-drive track going off to the south (left), a short distance from the falls. Continue on the Uloola Track past Uloola Swamp ❺ and the sandstone outcrop, 'Callaghans Tor' ❻ to Waterfall Oval, ignoring the Couranga Track ❼ going off to the east (left). Here the heath includes the rare mallee Yellow-top Ash as well as more familiar species such as Heath Banksia. The memorial at ❽ commemorates firefighters who perished fighting bushfires in the park. For a direct route to Waterfall Station, cross the oval.

Doing this walk in the reverse direction is a good option in warmer weather, as Karloo pool can be made a swimming as well as a lunch spot 🍎.

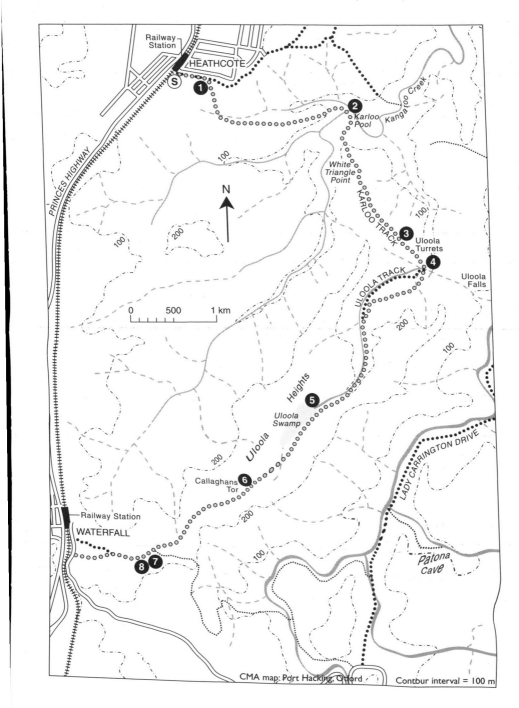

Railway Station

HEATHCOTE

S

1

Karloo Pool

Kangaroo Creek

2

White Triangle Point

100

KARLOO TRACK

100

N

200

100

3

Uloola Turrets

ULOOLA TRACK

4

Uloola Falls

200

0   500   1 km

100

Uloola Heights

5

Uloola Swamp

200

Uloola

LADY CARRINGTON DRIVE

Callaghans Tor

6

PRINCES HIGHWAY

200

Railway Station

WATERFALL

100

100

8 7

200

Patona Cave

CMA map: Port Hacking, Otford

Contour interval = 100 m

Heathcote Station – Kangaroo Creek – Karloo Pool

Don't miss this little gem in the Royal National Park, which features a pool-strewn creek and varied vegetation

- **Length:** 7½ km
- **Time from CBD:** 1 hour; rail access
- **Duration:** Short day
- **Children:** 9 years+

- **Nearest Refreshment:** Heathcote
- **Water:** Carry water
- **Toilets:** Heathcote Station (might be locked when station unattended)

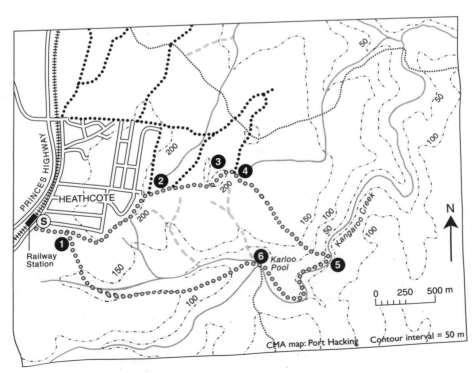

Near Karloo Pool

- **Track:** Little signposting; 4 km unconstructed; generally obvious; uneven and steep in places; no facilities; moderate–high use

- **Ups 'n' downs:** One steep ascent (120 in 1100 m); one steep descent (150 in 600 m)

- **Start:** Eastern side of Heathcote Railway Station.

TRACK NOTES

- Walk down the southern (right-hand) side of the Emergency Services compound and along the fire trail to the east. Ignore the Karloo Pool Track on the right about 350 m from the start ❶. Continue along the fire trail, turning right at the locked gate ❷. The quarry ❸ on the left was a source of laterite, a gravel used as a surfacing material, formed from the Wianamatta shale that once capped the area. In the surrounding medium eucalypt forest, Waratah and Gymea Lily flourish. At the next two track junctions (the last marked with a sign 'Audley') ❹, take the right-hand option.

- Follow the last 500 m of the fire trail and take (*with care*) the track to Kangaroo Creek ❺. Look out for Gymea Lily, and note the colourful Smooth-barked Apple, a feature of the medium eucalypt forest along the winding creek.

- At the creek, turn south-west (right) and proceed along the track to Karloo Pool ❻ for morning tea or lunch and possibly a swim ⬤. Note the rock platforms and pools along the creek.

- From Karloo Pool take the track to the north (right) back to Heathcote Station.

Doing this walk in the reverse direction is not recommended because the track up from Kangaroo Creek is hard to find.

No. 17

Walumarra Track –
Forest Path

*Abundant subtropical rainforest is encountered
along this Royal National Park track
located near Waterfall*

- **Length:** 13 km; or finish at ⑤, 8 km;
  or do the Forest Island circuit from ⑤,
  4 km

- **Time from CBD:** 1 hour

- **Duration:** Day (shorter options)

- **Children:** 9 years+

- **Nearest Refreshment:** Heathcote

- **Water:** Waterfall Station (might be
  locked when station unattended); Audley.
  Carry water

- **Toilets:** As for water

- **Track:** Some signposting; 1½ km

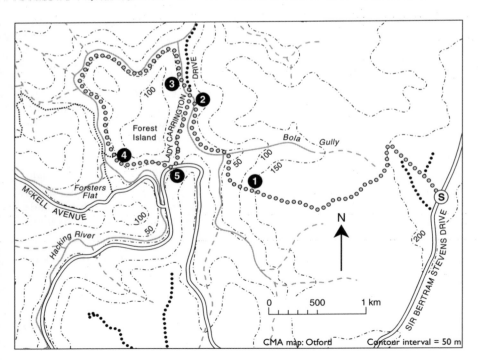

CMA map: Otford   Contour interval = 50 m

Sydney Peppermint, *Eucalyptus piperita*

unconstructed; obvious; uneven in places; some facilities; moderate–high use

- **Ups 'n' downs:** One steep ascent (140 in 800 m); one steep descent (140 in 800 m)

- **Start:** Walumarra Track car park on Sir Bertram Stevens Dr.

TRACK NOTES

◆ Take the fire trail from the car park, passing the Garie Trig Track branching to the north (right) about 250 m from the start. Continue on the trail to where it becomes a track. Along the way, enjoy views of the park and Sydney skyline, and heath vegetation.

◆ Follow the track through the cliff line ❶ to Bola Creek for a delightful experience of subtropical rainforest 🍎.

◆ Continue on across the creek to Lady Carrington Dr ❷. Turn north (right) and follow the road for about 100 m to where it is joined on the west (left) by the Forest Island Path ❸. Take this track all the way around Forest Island to Sir Bertram Stevens Dr. The rainforest and tall eucalypt forest which gives Forest Island its name include the easily recognised Cabbage Tree Palm and Blackbutt. A track coming in from the west (right) ❹ goes to Waterfall.

◆ Walk 700 m east to where Lady Carrington Dr joins Sir Betram Stevens Dr ❺. Follow Lady Carrington Dr for about 700 m to its junction with the Walumarra Track ❷. Retrace your steps up the Walumarra Track to the car park.

No. 18

Waterfall Station – Heathcote Station via the Bullawarring Track

Highlights of this popular hike in Heathcote National Park include several tranquil pools and a variety of forest and heath vegetation

♦ **Length:** 12 km; or to Kingfisher Pool return, 5 km; or ❶ to ❸, returning on the Mooray Track, 7½ km

♦ **Time from CBD:** 1 hour; rail access

♦ **Duration:** Day

♦ **Children:** 9 years+

♦ **Nearest Refreshment:** Heathcote

♦ **Water:** Waterfall and Heathcote stations (could be locked when station unattended). Carry water

♦ **Toilets:** As for water

♦ **Track:** Some signposting; 9 km unconstructed; obvious; uneven in places; no facilities; moderate–high use

♦ **Ups 'n' downs:** Two steep ascents (50 in 200 m, 100 in 1200 m); two steep descents (90 in 800 m, 50 in 200 m)

♦ **Start:** Car park on eastern side of Waterfall Railway Station. Travel by train from the end of the walk (Heathcote) to the start.

TRACK NOTES

♦ At the station exit turn west (right) and walk 200 m to Warabin St. Turn right and follow the street to its end ❶, where a fire trail goes off to the west (left). Proceed along the trail for about 50 m and take the track which branches off to the west (left) to the ford ❷ across Heathcote Creek.

♦ After crossing the ford, take the track to the north-east (right), following it through medium eucalypt forest past Bondel and Kingfisher pools to Myuna Pool and the junction with the Mooray Track ❸. Nearby on the creek are good spots for an eating stop.

♦ Continue left along the track away from Heathcote Creek, across a small side-creek and up the ridge to a natural lookout on a rock shelf ❹. From here continue north for about 1¼ km to a track junction ❺. Keep a look out for Gymea Lily along this part of the walk.

♦ From the junction take the left-hand track, crossing the ridge and then descending to the Pipeline Rd and the pipeline from Woronora Dam. Turn

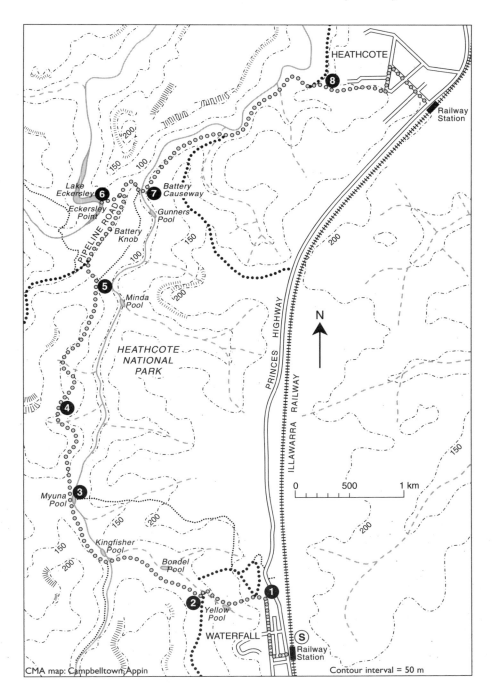

HEATHCOTE

Railway
Station

Lake
Eckersley

Battery
Causeway

Eckersley
Point

Gunners
Pool

Battery
Knob

PIPELINE ROAD

Minda
Pool

HEATHCOTE
NATIONAL
PARK

N

PRINCES HIGHWAY

ILLAWARRA RAILWAY

0   500   1 km

Myuna
Pool

Kingfisher
Pool

Bondel
Pool

Yellow
Pool

WATERFALL

S
Railway
Station

CMA map: Campbelltown, Appin

Contour interval = 50 m

north-east (right) and follow the road for about 1 km. A sign on a pipeline support indicates a rough and indistinct track to Lake Eckersley on the left. A clearer track is 150 m farther. Descend to the lake **6** for lunch and a swim.

♦ Return to the pipeline road, turn left and follow it down to, and across Battery Causeway **7**. Continue for another 2 km to a metal bridge over the pipeline **8**. Cross the bridge and follow the track up Scout Gully to the Scouts Association camp site. A track to Boundary Rd, Heathcote, goes through the camp — or an alternative route, avoiding the camp, involves taking the track branching off to the right from the area where there is a fireplace and terraced seating. In one place, the alternative track is indistinct. It can be picked up again by turning right and crossing a small rise. Heathcote Station can be reached by following Boundary Rd and Oliver St.

Kingfisher Pool, Bullawarring Track

Walks in the Lower Blue Mountains (West)

The plateau surface of the Lower Blue Mountains has been eroded into a tangle of valleys and ridges. The walks in this group sample this delightful and interesting country. Several of the walks — 19, 20, 21, 24 and 25 — follow or include a visit to a creek, some offering swimming opportunities. Walks 19 and 25 pass through cool, moist gully forest, while a feature of walk 24 is a beautiful forest of Sydney Blue Gum. Walk 24 also includes a visit to a lookout above the gorge of the lower Grose River. The steep, gorge-like valley of the Colo River is viewed on walk 23 and is actually entered on walk 22. A highlight of walk 20 is a visit to an Aboriginal cultural site. Wildflower displays, in season, can be expected on all of these walks.

No. 19

Florabella Pass

Excellent bird life, creek views, open forest and gully vegetation are highlights of this Blue Mountains National Park walk starting at Warrimoo

◆ **Length:** 7 km

◆ **Time from CBD**: 1 hour; rail access

◆ **Duration:** Short day

◆ **Children:** 9 years+

◆ **Nearest Refreshment:** Blaxland

◆ **Water:** Blaxland and Warrimoo rail stations; Blaxland Mall. Carry water

◆ **Toilets:** As for water

◆ **Track:** Some signposting; mainly unconstructed; obvious; some steps; no facilities; moderate–high use

◆ **Ups 'n' downs:** Three steep ascents (70 in 300 m, 40 in 100 m, 60 in 100 m); one moderate ascent (60 in 800 m); two steep descents (100 in 200 m, 60 in 100 m); one moderate descent (70 in 400 m)

◆ **Start:** Warrimoo Rail Station or the end of Florabella St. It is recommended that car travellers leave their car at Blaxland (the finish of the walk) and take the train to Warrimoo.

TRACK NOTES

◆ From the station, walk west before turning south (left) into The Boulevard. Turn right into Arthur St and then left into Florabella St. The track actually starts to the left of the sign 'Florabella Pass' at the end of Florabella St and passes initially through medium-low eucalypt forest, in which Smooth-barked Apple and Old Man Banksia are evident, before descending into an area of gully forest.

◆ Follow the track past some rock overhangs down to, and across Florabella Creek. From here the track climbs away from the Creek, but returns to it after about 900 m. Bird life in this section is a feature. Be on the lookout especially for Crimson Rosella and Lyrebird.

◆ The path will then take you on the eastern (left-hand) side of the creek, across a bridge ❶ and on to a large overhang ❷ 🍎. Note the pothole in the bed of the creek and the honeycomb weathering of the sandstone in the overhang.

◆ Continue along the track across a rock shelf above Glenbrook Creek and a small side-stream. About 500 m beyond the overhang, locate the secondary track off to the west (right) and proceed down it to Glenbrook Creek. At the Creek, turn north (right) and follow the Creek upstream to a pool ❸ 🍎.

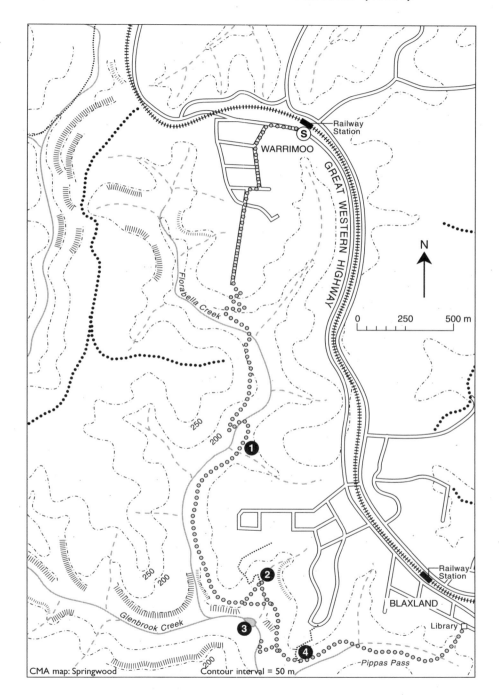

CMA map: Springwood

Contour interval = 50 m

◆ Return to the main track, turning south (right). Follow the track past the junction with Pippas Track at ➍ and on along the valley through gully forest to the end of the track behind the library at Blaxland.

Tall eucalypt forest, Blue Mountains National Park

Glenbrook Causeway – Red Hands Cave

This popular creek walk in the Blue Mountains National Park includes ancient Aboriginal stencil paintings

- **Length:** 8 km; or return from ❸, 6 km; or car pick-up at ❸, 3 km

- **Time from CBD**: 1½ hours; rail access

- **Duration:** Short day

- **Children:** 9 years+

- **Nearest Refreshment:** Glenbrook

- **Water:** Glenbrook Station; Red Hands Cave car park; Park entrance. Carry water

- **Toilets:** As for water

- **Track:** Some signposting; mainly unconstructed; generally obvious; many uneven steps; no facilities; moderate–high use

- **Ups 'n' downs:** One steep ascent (25 in 100 m); one steep descent (90 in 400 m)

- **Start:** Glenbrook Creek causeway on road into the Blue Mountains National Park at Glenbrook. If travelling by car, turn at the National Park sign on the Great Western Hwy and follow the road past the Park entrance, across the causeway, and up the hill to the car park at the second hairpin bend. Use the steps to return to the causeway. If travelling by train, turn right at exit from station and follow road into the National Park for 1½ km (walk to start involves a steep descent of 100 m and the corresponding ascent on the return journey).

TRACK NOTES

- From the causeway, look for the sign at the beginning of the track along Camp Fire Creek ❶.

- Follow this track, which stays on the south (left) side of the creek, upstream or in a south-westerly direction to the spot ❷ where Camp Fire Creek is joined by a smaller creek coming in from the west (the right) and a turn-off is indicated by a signpost. The vegetation along these creeks is mainly medium eucalypt forest, with its typical diversity of flora including Sydney Peppermint, Smooth-barked Apple, Christmas Bush, Water Gum and Graceful Bush-pea.

- Turn north-west (right) off the track you are on, cross Camp Fire Creek and join the track that follows the smaller creek. You may be fortunate enough to see freshwater crayfish or yabbies as you cross the creek.

- This track climbs steadily through the medium eucalypt forest. Follow it as it stays close to the creek, up to Red

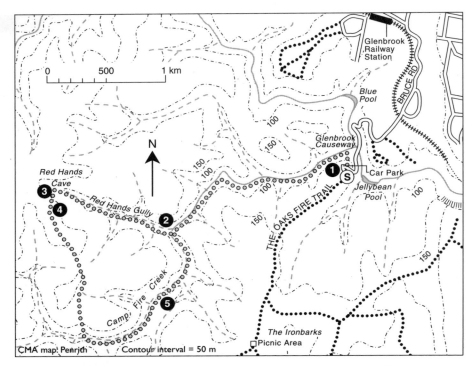

Scale: 0   500   1 km

CMA map: Penrith   Contour interval = 50 m

Hands Cave ❸. A good spot for a sit-down break (and a morning-tea or lunch 🍎) is on the flat rock above the cave. The stencil paintings in the cave are from an Aboriginal culture dating back 12 000 years. Note the outline of a child's hand on the left side of the back wall of the cave.

◆ Take the track up the slope to the Red Hands Cave car park ❹. Continue south through the open forest for a little over a kilometre and then make the steep descent to Camp Fire Creek. *Take care on the steep bit if the track is at all wet.*

◆ At the creek turn east (left) and follow the path to the junction at Red Hands Gully ❷. Signs indicate the location of Aboriginal sharpening grooves in flat rocks along the creek ❺.

◆ From the junction, return along the Camp Fire Creek Track to the Glenbrook Creek causeway.

No. 21

Erskine Creek – Pisgah Rock – Jack Evans Track

Enjoy diverse vegetation on this short, two-part walk in the Blue Mountains National Park near Glenbrook

- **Length:** 4 km; or just Part 1, 1½ km; or just Part 2, 3 km
- **Time from CBD:** 1½ hours
- **Duration:** Short day

- **Children:** 7 years+
- **Nearest Refreshment:** Glenbrook
- **Water:** Oaks picnic area. Carry water
- **Toilets:** Glenbrook Station; Red Hands Cave car park; Park entrance
- **Track:** Some signposting; unconstructed (some development); obvious; uneven in places; no facilities; moderate–high use
- **Ups 'n' downs:** One moderate descent and ascent (170 in 1400 m)
- **Start:** Car park for the Pisgah Rock Track. From the Glenbrook entrance to the National Park, cross the Glenbrook Creek causeway and take the Oaks Fire Trail and turn left just beyond the Oaks picnic area into the Nepean Lookout Trail. The car park is 2 km from the junction, on the left.

TRACK NOTES

This is a two-part walk, each part providing a different experience of the picturesque Erskine Creek.

♦ From the car park ❶, cross the road and follow the track the 750 m to Pisgah Rock ❷ for views of Erskine and Lincoln creeks. In the surrounding

River Rose, *Bauera rubioides*

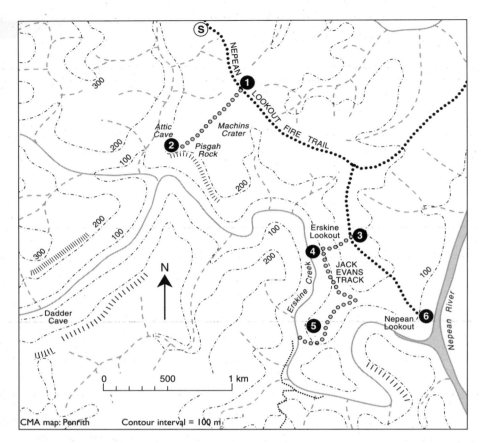

CMA map: Penrith   Contour interval = 100 m

medium eucalypt forest, Black She-oak, Woody Pear and Bloodwoods are much in evidence.

◆ Return to your car and drive to the Jack Evans Track car park ❸. Take the track south-west from the car park deviating right after about 300 m to gain another elevated view of Erskine Creek from ❹. Continue down the well-graded track to a pool in Erskine Creek ❺ 🍎, noting the many specimens of Grass-tree along the way.

◆ Time can be spent swimming and/or exploring upstream and downstream from ❺. Do this on rock platforms — for example, upstream on the eastern side — and where there is a track. (The track going downstream from where the Jack Evans Track crosses Erskine Creek goes to the creek's junction with the Nepean River. Although only 2½ km in length, this track is very difficult in places, and is only for seasoned walkers with several hours to spare.)

◆ Return to the car by the same route. A drive to the Nepean Lookout ❻ is recommended.

Bob Turner Track

*The highlight of this walk in Wollemi National Park
near Colo Heights is a beautiful pool in
a steep-sided gorge*

- ◆ **Length:** 7 km
- ◆ **Time from CBD**: 2 hours
- ◆ **Duration:** Short day
- ◆ **Children:** 9 years+
- ◆ **Nearest Refreshment:** Windsor
- ◆ **Toilets:** Colo Park (at Colo River Bridge). Carry water

- ◆ **Track:** Signposting; unconstructed (some development); obvious; a few uneven patches; no facilities; moderate–high use
- ◆ **Ups 'n' downs:** Three short very steep descents and ascents; several moderate ascents and descents (overall descent/ascent — 240 m)
- ◆ **Start:** Fire trail to the track head ❶,

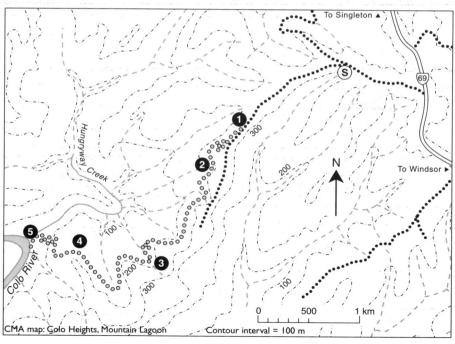

CMA map: Colo Heights, Mountain Lagoon   Contour interval = 100 m

which leaves the Putty Rd 16.3 km from the Colo River Bridge. An Ampol service station on the right, 700 m before the turn-off, is a useful marker. The fire trail is signposted as 'Bob Turner Track 3 km'. The track head is also clearly signposted and is located in a saddle, where several cars can be parked.

TRACK NOTES

Ideally, do this walk in swimming, but NOT hot, weather; that is, during late spring or early autumn.

◆ The track goes north-east from ❶ for a metre or two before turning south-east. Apart from three zig-zag sections it maintains a generally south-easterly or easterly direction for its entire length. The track is very easy to follow to its end at a scenically beautiful pool in the Colo River ❺ ●. The varied medium eucalypt forest reflects changing moisture and soil conditions. Geebung (Pine-Leaf and Broad-Leaf), Tea-tree, Mountain Devil, Banksia and other sclerophyllous species dominate. There is a vigorous specimen of Lawyer Vine at ❸. At ❹ there is a large stand of Grey Ironbark, and Burrawang and Grass-tree also occur here. In summer, Christmas Bush and Fringed Lily ❷ are a special treat.

◆ When the river is at its normal level, the pool is ideal for swimming, the beach providing a sandy and gently sloping place to enter. *Check the situation, however, because floods can change the nature of the beach quite dramatically.* Spend time here to savour the grandeur of the V-shaped Colo River gorge, the fringing forest of River She-oak, and the Water Gum behind the beach.

◆ The return walk takes slightly longer than 1½ hours.

Flannel Flower, *Actinotus helianthi*

Mountain Lagoon – Colo River Gorge Viewpoint

Enjoy the Wollemi National Park's beautiful tall forest and its views of the Colo River Gorge and the ridges and peaks of the Wollemi and Yengo National Parks

- **Length:** 11 km
- **Time from CBD**: 2 hours
- **Duration:** Short day
- **Children:** 9 years+
- **Nearest Refreshment:** Bilpin
- **Water:** Carry water
- **Toilets:** None
- **Track:** Signposting; constructed (road); obvious; even surface; no facilities; low–moderate use
- **Ups 'n' downs:** One moderate descent and ascent (40 in 900 m)
- **Start:** Sams Way at Mountain Lagoon. The turn-off (on the right) to Mountain Lagoon is 25 km along Bells Line of Road from the Hawkesbury River Bridge at North Richmond. Follow the Mountain Lagoon Rd for 12.7 km to the signposted left turn into Sams Way. Follow Sams Way for 1.3 km to a NPWS sign 'Tootie Creek — Colo Meroo', indicating the start of the track on the northern (left-hand) side of the road.

TRACK NOTES

- Follow the track for 500 m to a sign-posted Y-junction ❶. Take the left-hand fork marked 'Tootie Creek 4 km'. The magnificent tall eucalypt forest here includes Round-leaved Blue Gum, Turpentine, Stringybark, Smooth-barked Apple and Grass-tree.

- About 900 m further there is another junction ❸. Ignore the management track and take the right-hand option. Note the tree ferns along the way.

- Continue for about 4 km to the car-turning area marking the end of the road. Note the sign indicating the track to the Tootie Creek — Colo River junction. The first viewpoint ❹ is about 50 m along this track 🍎. A second viewpoint ❺ is about 40 m further. Keep a look out for termite (not ant) mounds along the eastern (right-hand) side of the road through this medium eucalypt forest. The panorama includes the Colo River Gorge (east) and the ridges and peaks of the Wollemi and Yengo national parks (west, north-west).

- Return by the same route.

The map for walk 23 is on page 98.

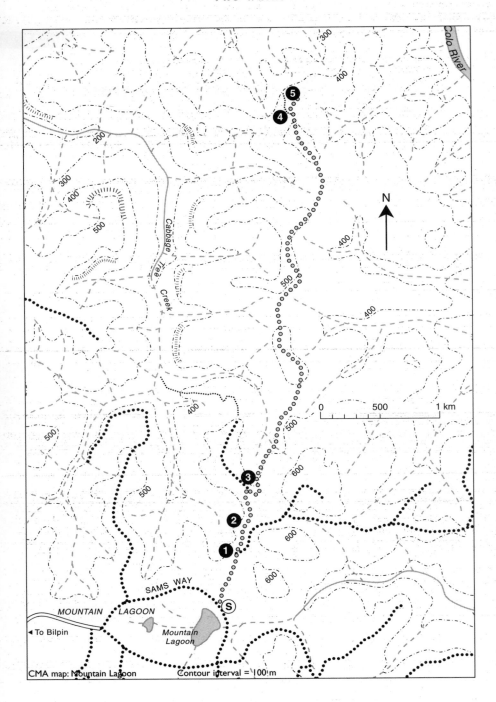

CMA map: Mountain Lagoon Contour interval = 100 m

No. 24

Winmalee – Shaws Ridge – Grose Mountain Lookout

This Blue Mountains National Park track features a stately tall forest and a view of the Grose River Gorge

- **Length:** 15 km; or omit the Lookout ascent, 10 km

- **Time from CBD:** 1½ hours

- **Duration:** Day

- **Children:** 11 years+

- **Nearest Refreshment:** Winmalee

- **Water:** Carry water

- **Toilets:** Winmalee Shopping Centre

- **Track:** Some signposting; 400 m unconstructed; obvious; loose gravel surface in places; some facilities; moderate–high use

- **Ups 'n' downs:** Three moderate ascents (30 in 600 m, 140 in 1600 m, 70 in 400 m); three moderate descents (80 in 800 m, 70 in 400 m, 140 in 1600)

- **Start:** End of White Cross Rd ❶, Winmalee. Turn north off Hawkesbury Rd at Winmalee Shopping Centre.

TRACK NOTES

- From ❶, follow the fire trail for 150 m to the first junction ❷. Take the trail to the north (right) and follow it to a second junction ❸ and the 'Shaws Ridge' signpost. Turn west (left) to take the ridge-top trail through medium eucalypt forest.

The map for walk 24 is on page 100.

- After about 3½ km, the trail descends steeply to Blue Gum Swamp Creek, so named for the abundance of tall, stately Round-leaved Blue Gum. From the foot of the descent, follow the trail for about 500 m to a picnic area ❹.

- About 200 m beyond the picnic area, take the road going off to the west (right) ❺. When the Springwood Ridge trail is reached, turn north (right) and continue on to the Grose Mountain Lookout ❻ 🍎 for a view of the Cumberland Plain and of the 'bottle-necked' Grose River Gorge.

- A side-trip to Grose Head South (1½ km return) will provide good views west up the Grose Valley.

- Retrace your steps along the Springwood Ridge Fire Trail, taking care to turn south (left) to rejoin the Blue Gum Swamp Creek Trail. At ❺, turn south (right) for the walk along the creek and back to the start via a second picnic area ❼. The 1 km return trip along the track going off to south-west (right) at ❼ is worth taking in order to visit the 'Grotto' ❽, a cool, peaceful place. Back on the main track, turn south (right) at ❷ to return to the start.

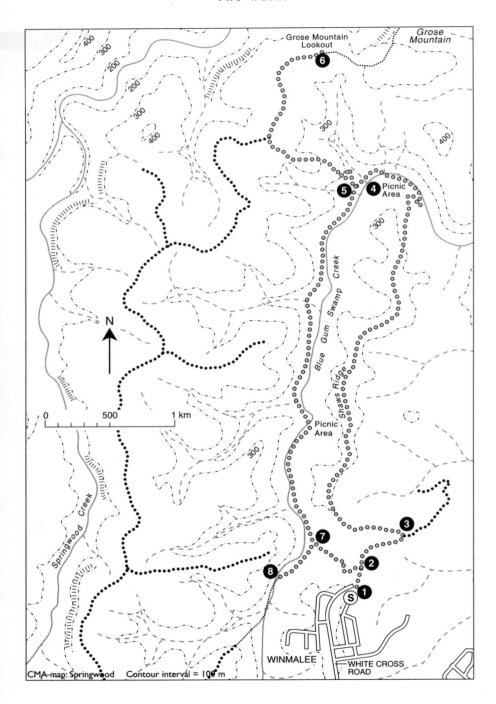

Magdala Creek –
Glenbrook Creek – Sassafras Creek

Visit several waterfalls and pools along picturesque creeks in the Blue Mountains National Park near Springwood

♦ **Length:** 11 km; or from Bee Farm Road via Wiggins Track to ❾ return, 3 km; or from Valley Rd to ❾, returning on track to Sassafras Gully Rd, 6 km

♦ **Time from CBD:** 1½ hours; rail access

♦ **Duration:** Short day

♦ **Children:** 9 years+

♦ **Nearest Refreshment:** Springwood

♦ **Water:** Carry water

♦ **Toilets:** Rest Park, Macquarie St, Springwood; Springwood Station

♦ **Track:** Some signposting; 10 km unconstructed; obvious; some uneven surfaces; some facilities; moderate–high use

♦ **Ups 'n' downs:** One steep ascent (100 in 400 m)

♦ **Start:** Springwood Station or Picnic Point, which is at the end of Valley Rd. Leave cars in Valley Rd or Picnic Glen St.

TRACK NOTES

♦ Exit the station and cross Macquarie St (the main street) and go through the car park to Springwood Ave. Take the Fairy Dell Track, which begins opposite the car park and next to the Scout

The map for walk 25 is on page 102.

Hall. About 400 m along, the Fairy Dell Track joins the Magdala Creek Track, which starts from Picnic Point.

♦ If starting from Picnic Point, go to the north-east corner of the grassy clearing to find the beginning of the Magdala Creek Track. At the junction with the Fairy Dell Track turn south (right). Proceed straight ahead (south), ignoring the track on the east (left) to Lawsons Lookout, about 150 m farther on. Near the start of the Lawsons Lookout Track, a sign is being enveloped by a Smooth-barked Apple.

♦ The track follows Magdala Ck, crossing it several times. *Exercise great care where the track is on rock, as the surface can be very slippery.* Stay with the track all the way to Perch Ponds ❽, ignoring the tracks going off to the left at ❷ and ❺ and to the right at ❸. The gully forest here features some fine specimens of Turpentine, rock overhangs, especially at ❹, Magdala Falls and Blue Pool ❻ and Martin Falls ❼.

♦ At Perch Ponds, take the track to the north-west (right), up Glenbrook Creek to its junction with Sassafras Creek and a delightful, swimmable pool ●.

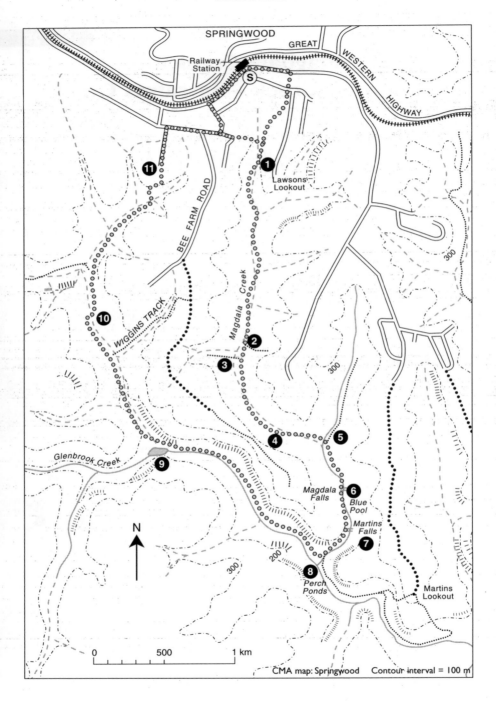

SPRINGWOOD

GREAT WESTERN HIGHWAY

Railway Station

S

1

Lawsons Lookout

11

BEE FARM ROAD

10

WIGGINS TRACK

Magdala Creek

2

3

300

300

4

5

6

Magdala Falls

Blue Pool

Martins Falls

7

Glenbrook Creek

9

N

200

8

300

Perch Ponds

Martins Lookout

0   500   1 km

CMA map: Springwood   Contour interval = 100 m

◆ Continue along the track, which now follows Sassafras Creek, where the gully forest is particularly attractive. Ignore the Wiggins Track going off the north-east (right). At the arrow sign **10**, indicating that the track takes a sharp right turn into the creek, cross the creek in the direction of the arrow — don't turn up the creek. Proceed on to where the Victoria Track joins from the west (left).

◆ From the Victoria Track junction, go straight on (north-east) up to Sassafras Gully Rd, pausing to observe the memorial to 'Paddy' **11**.

Willow-leaved Crowea, *Crowea saligna*

Walks in the
Upper Blue Mountains
(West)

Much of the first walk in this group is through gully forest and visits a number of waterfalls and pools. The remainder of the walks offer rather different attractions, although waterfalls are a feature of walks 33 and 34 and especially walks 27, 29 and 31. The most commanding and famous of these attractions are cliff and valley panoramas, but there is so much more to be seen on the walks — rainforest, tall forest, canyons, rock overhangs and caves and abundant bird life, to list just a few features. Walk 35 visits the very different terrain of the Coxs River Valley. Although farther afield than most of the other walks in this group, walk 38 is not to be missed. Apart from the fascinating railway history that it recalls, it is brimful of exciting features including a walk through an abandoned tunnel colonised by glow worms.

Hazelbrook Station – Hazelbrook Lake (Bedford Pool)

Waterfalls, pools and delightful forest vegetation are featured on this outing in the Blue Mountains National Park

◆ **Length:** 10 km; or turn left at **7** and return to start via Baths Rd, 6 km; or start from **13** and walk to **12** and **11**, returning via **10** and **9**, then turn right at **8** for the walk to **13**, 3 km.

◆ **Time from CBD**: 1½ hours; rail access

◆ **Duration:** Day

◆ **Children:** 9 years+

◆ **Nearest Refreshment:** Hazelbrook

◆ **Water:** Carry water

◆ **Toilets:** Hazelbrook Station (might be closed)

◆ **Track:** Some signposting; 3 km unconstructed; obvious; rough, steep and slippery in places; no facilities; low–moderate use

◆ **Ups 'n' downs:** One steep ascent (90 in 350 m); several moderate ascents and descents

◆ **Start:** Hazelbrook Railway Station or, if travelling by car, the corner of Terrace Falls Rd and Baths Rd, Hazelbrook.

TRACK NOTES

◆ From the station, walk west along Railway Pde to Baths Rd via Terrace Falls Rd. From Baths Rd follow Broad St to its junction with Livingstone Rd **1**. Take the path leading off to the south (left) and follow it to the base of Adelina Falls **2**, noting the lovely ferns including King Fern.

◆ Return to the track and continue on through gully forest to Junction Falls **3**. Back on the track again, proceed to where steps go up to the left. Go straight on for about 150 m for a view of Federal Falls **4**. Return to the steps and make your way to Cataract Falls **5** and the lookout **6** just to the west of the falls.

◆ From Cataract Falls, take the fire trail to the south-east (right). Turn south (right) where the fire trail from Baths Rd is joined **7**. After about 1 km, a junction is reached. Ignore the track that goes straight on (south), but take the main track north-east and down the hill to a ford. Just beyond the ford, locate the narrower track to the south (right) **8**. Follow this track into the valley through gully forest to Victor Falls **9** and Terrace Falls **10**, looking out for plant species markers.

◆ Cross the creek at Terrace Falls and follow the track as it crosses the creek

The walks

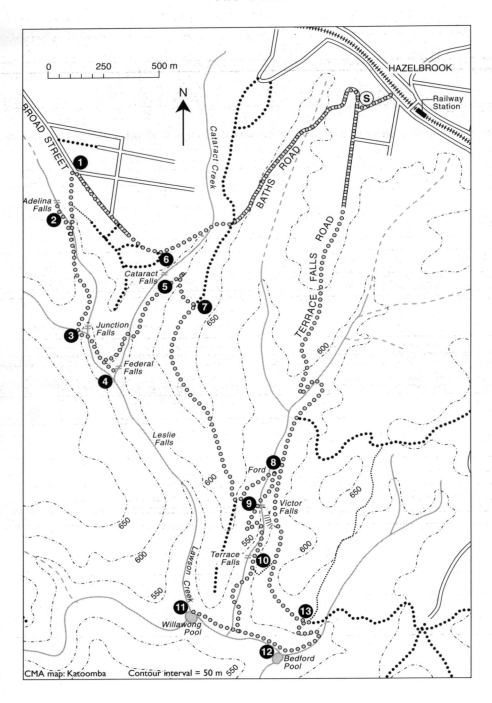

0   250   500 m

N

BROAD STREET

Adelina Falls

Cataract Creek

HAZELBROOK

Railway Station

BATHS ROAD

TERRACE FALLS ROAD

S

Cataract Falls

Junction Falls

Federal Falls

Leslie Falls

Ford

Victor Falls

Terrace Falls

Lawson Creek

Willawong Pool

Bedford Pool

650

600

600

650

600

550

550

600

650

550

550

CMA map: Katoomba   Contour interval = 50 m

1 2 3 4 5 6 7 8 9 10 11 12 13

twice more and takes you to Bedford Creek and the remains of a bridge. A lesser track going off to the left near Terrace Falls should be ignored. At the track junction, take the right-hand option for a return walk to Willawong Pool **❶❶**. Return to the junction, going straight on to Bedford Pool (Lake Hazelbrook) **❶❷** 🍎— a good spot for a swim in warm weather.

◆ Follow the track away from the creek and up the side of the valley to a fire trail and car park **❶❸**. Turn west (left) and follow the trail to Terrace Falls Rd for the walk back to the start.

Empress Falls, Valley of the Waters

No. 27

Wentworth Falls Amphitheatre

Marvel at vast panoramas, majestic cliffs and
waterfalls on this classic walk in the
Blue Mountains National Park

♦ **Length:** 5 km; or 10½ km if starting and
finishing at Wentworth Falls Railway
Station; or the 'Shortcut Track' from
NPWS building to join 'Undercliff/
Overcliff Track', 3 km

♦ **Time from CBD:** 2 hours; rail access

♦ **Duration:** Short day

♦ **Children:** 9 years+

♦ **Nearest Refreshment:** Wentworth
Falls

♦ **Water:** NPWS building, Wentworth Falls
Picnic Area. Carry water

♦ **Toilets:** As for water

♦ **Track:** Signposting; mainly unconstructed;
obvious; steps, stairs, muddy sections;
some facilities; moderate–high use

♦ **Ups 'n' downs:** One moderate/steep
descent (200 in 500 m); one steep/very
steep ascent (200 in 600 m)

♦ **Start:** There are two possibilities: (a)
NPWS building (Conservation Hut) at
the western end of Fletcher St,
Wentworth Falls; *or* (b) Wentworth Falls
Railway Station. To get to the NPWS
building from the station, walk south to
the Great Western Hwy. Cross, turn right
and proceed to Falls Rd, the first street
on the left. Fletcher St is the third street
on the right along Falls Rd.

TRACK NOTES

♦ From the car park, follow the track
marked by 'National Pass' signs to
Queen Victoria Lookout ❶. From here,
the view takes in the Valley of the
Waters, part of the Jamison and the
eastern end of Mount Solitary. The
rocks in the very bottom of the valley
are up to 300 million years old.

♦ Continue along the track to Empress
Lookout and then down the metal
stairs to the base of Empress Falls ❷,
passing the nature trail going off to the
north (right). The vegetation type
changes abruptly from low eucalypt to
gully forest.

♦ The track crosses the creek below
Empress Falls but returns to the
eastern (left-hand side) above Ladore
Falls ❸. The passage through the
Valley of the Waters is scenically stun-
ning and provides more views of the
Jamison Valley.

♦ At the signposted junction with the
Wentworth Pass Track, continue south-
east along the National Pass to the
rocky outcrop at ❹ 🍎 for a superb
view of the Wentworth Falls. The vegetation here includes the very rare,
mallee-like Bäuerlen's Gum, pockets of
fern, sedges and Christmas Bell.

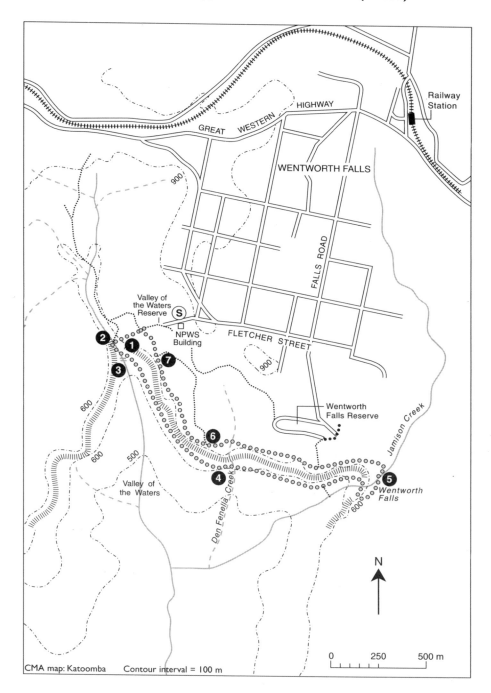

Valley of
the Waters
Reserve

NPWS
Building

Wentworth
Falls Reserve

Valley of
the Waters

Wentworth
Falls

N

CMA map: Katoomba   Contour interval = 100 m

0   250   500 m

◆ Continue on the National Pass to the base of the upper Wentworth Falls ⚫, ignoring the track to Slacks Stairs going off to the south (right). The vegetation growing on the cliff face in the spray of the falls includes some rare species, most notably the Dwarf Pine. The view of the Jamison Valley and Mount Solitary from the base of the falls is spectacular.

◆ The track climbs steeply from here and, in places, consists of stairs cut into the cliff face. The track crosses Jamison Creek at the top of the Falls and near Queens Cascades. Take the stairs and, just past Weeping Rock ❺, turn west (left) onto the Undercliff Track. Disregard track branches on the right (unless you wish to take a shorter return route to the station via Wentworth Falls Reserve and Falls Rd).

◆ Turn left at the track junction near Den Fenella Ck and cross the bridge. You are now on the Overcliff Walk. The side-tracks to the south (left) go to lookouts which are worth visiting.

◆ Continue on to Breakfast Point Lookout ❻. From here you can turn right and take the track that goes directly to the NPWS building. Otherwise, stay on the Overcliff Walk for wonderful valley views. Just beyond Lyrebird Lookout ❼, the track veers away from the cliff and climbs to meet the Valley of the Waters Track. At the junction, turn east (right) to return to the NPWS hut.

Sylvia Falls, Wentworth Falls Ampitheatre walk

No. 28

Mount Hay Road – Lockley Pylon – Du Faur Head

As well as superb views, this track in the Blue Mountains National Park north of Leura features interesting heath vegetation

- **Length:** 8 km
- **Time from CBD:** 2 hours; car access
- **Duration:** Short day
- **Children:** 9 years+
- **Nearest Refreshment:** Leura
- **Water:** Carry water
- **Toilets:** Leura shopping centre car park (left off main street)
- **Track:** Some signposting; unconstructed except for some wooden stairways near end; generally obvious; mostly even, but narrow and stony in first ½ km; no facilities; moderate–high usage
- **Ups 'n' downs:** Mainly level with one moderate (70 in 500 m) and several short ascents and descents
- **Start:** The head of the Lockley Pylon Track Head on the Mount Hay Rd. Turn off Great Western Hwy at pedestrian overbridge ½ km east of traffic lights at Leura. The car park (signposted) at the track head is 10 km from the beginning of Mount Hay Rd. The road is mainly gravel and is narrow and steep in places.

TRACK NOTES

♦ From the car park, the track ascends slightly and then skirts along the west side of The Pinnacles, a narrow ridge topped by sandstone outcrops. The track is narrow and stony at first, splitting and rejoining once or twice. A short track ❶ branches to the summit of The Pinnacles, which affords a view down Fortress Creek, a valley 'hanging' above the much deeper valley beyond. The vegetation here is a mix of Blue Mountains Ash and shrub heath.

♦ Beyond The Pinnacles, the track descends and becomes wider and clearer. The peaks visible to the northwest and north are (from left to right) Hat Hill, Mount Banks, Mount Bell, Mount Tomah, Mount Caley and Mount Hay.

♦ The track rises and falls slightly before climbing to a rocky eminence ❸. Climb to the pagoda-like summit on the north (left) of the track for very fine views. Flannel Flower is abundant around the outcrop between October and January.

The walks

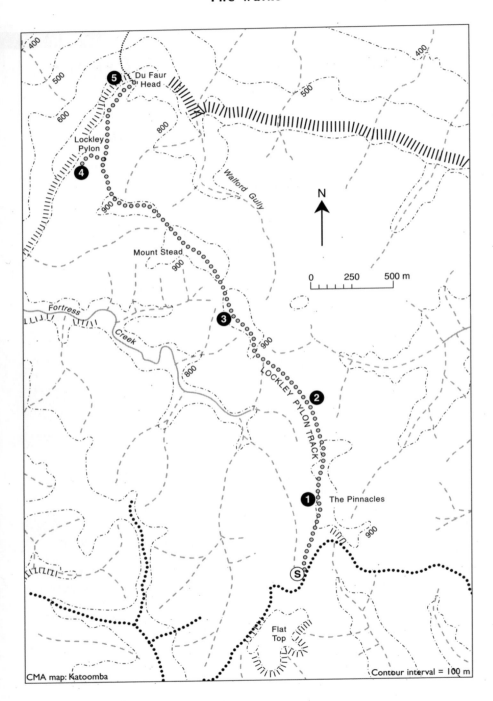

Du Faur Head

Lockley Pylon

Walford Gully

N

0   250   500 m

Fortress

Creek

Mount Stead

LOCKLEY PYLON TRACK

The Pinnacles

Flat Top

CMA map: Katoomba

Contour interval = 100 m

112

◆ After crossing several small rises, including Mount Stead, the track traverses an extensive heath area before reaching Lockley Pylon. Look out for the conspicuously flowering Blue Mint Bush along the rock ledges in October.

◆ The Lockley Pylon Track goes right over the summit to a point on the south-west side ❹ ⦿ providing spectacular views of the vast gorge of Govetts Creek and the Fortress Creek Falls emerging from cliffs on the left. *Take care because there is no safety fence here (and on Du Faur Head).* (In wet weather a dry spot can be found in a rock shelter just below and left of this.)

◆ The return to the main track is by the same route. To visit Du Faur Head turn north (left) at the junction. The track skirts the base of Lockley Pylon then descends steeply by wooden steps into the head of a gully, ascending again and crossing a narrow saddle onto Du Faur Head ❺. The views from here are of the upper and downstream valley of the Grose River. The basalt-capped peaks of Mount Banks, Mount Tomah, Mount Caley and Mount Hay will be obvious. Note the rare Cliff Mallee growing here.

◆ Return by the same route.

Track in cliff face above the Wentworth Falls

No. 29

Scenic Railway Picnic Area – Golden Stairs – Furber Stairs

Sweeping views, rainforest, and historical and geological features are among the highlights of this classic Blue Mountains National Park walk at Katoomba

- **Length:** 6½ km; or take the Scenic Railway ➏ to the car park, 5½ km

- **Time from CBD**: 2½ hours; rail access (with taxi)

- **Duration:** Short day (shorter/easier option)

- **Children:** 9 years+

- **Nearest Refreshment:** Katoomba

- **Water:** Carry water

- **Toilets:** Scenic Railway tourist complex and picnic area

- **Track:** Signposting; mainly constructed; obvious; some uneven surfaces; some facilities; high use

- **Ups 'n' downs:** One steep descent (160 in 800 m); one steep ascent (190 in 900 m); several short, moderate ascents and descents

- **Start:** Scenic Railway picnic area off Cliff Dr, Katoomba, 3 km from Katoomba Station. From the station, walk south down Katoomba St and turn right at Katoomba Falls Rd.

TRACK NOTES

- At the tourist complex, obtain a copy of the free *Blue Mountains Tourist Newspaper* (contains a useful guide) and pause to observe the birds, notably King Parrots. Exit the picnic area, turning left into Cliff Dr, which is followed for about 1 km to where Glenraphael Dr (signposted) goes off to the south (left) ➋. Because the verge of the road is narrow, *be alert for vehicles.* The short side-trip to the Landslide Lookout ➊ is recommended for views of Narrow Neck Plateau, Jamison Valley (south), and Megalong Valley (west), where the Coxs River has carved a valley in a valley.

- Follow Glenraphael Dr for 1¾ km to an information board and the steel 'Golden Stairs' signpost ➌ on the left. From here the Golden Stairs Track is followed to the Federal Pass Track ➍. The views of the landslides on the opposite cliff face are spectacular. The transition from low to tall eucalypt forest as the track descends is notable.

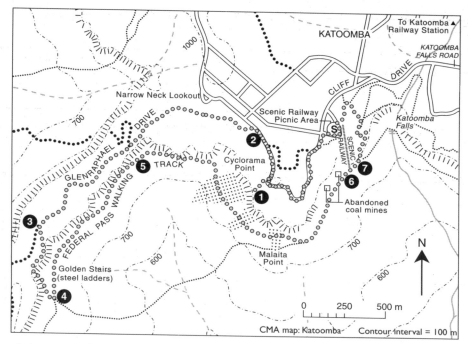

Map labels: To Katoomba ▲ Railway Station; KATOOMBA; KATOOMBA FALLS ROAD; Narrow Neck Lookout; CLIFF DRIVE; Scenic Railway Picnic Area; Katoomba Falls; GLENRAPHAEL DRIVE; TRACK; Cyclorama Point; FEDERAL PASS WALKING; SCENIC RAILWAY; Abandoned coal mines; Golden Stairs (steel ladders); Malaita Point; N; 0 250 500 m; CMA map: Katoomba Contour interval = 100 m

♦ Turn north (left) along the Federal Pass Track. Look out for the adit (entrance) of shale railway tunnel through Narrow Neck **5** ● Continue on through the warm-temperate rainforest, featuring Coachwood, Blackwattle and Black Sassafras, to the foot of the Furber Stairs **7**. For a complete guide to the metal markers along the track, consult the *Blue Mountains Tourist Newspaper*. A short guide is given below. *Across the scree of the landslides, use the track marked by steel poles.*

♦ Take the clearly signposted Furber Stairs Track to Scenic Railway car park, reading the signs and spotting birds such as Currawongs, King Parrots, Golden Whistlers and Yellow Robins.

Key to selected markers: Flora — F3 Blueberry Ash; F4 Rough Tree Fern; F8 Blackwattle; F11 Cedar Wattle; F12 Lilly-Pilly; F14 Scaly Tree Ferns (70–100 years old); F15 200–300-year-old Angophora; F16 Mountain Ash; F17 Forest Coachwood; F18 Sassafras; F20 Sydney Peppermint. **Geology —** G3 'natural' rock fall; G4 large rock fall (in three stages, Jan.–June 1931), the result of mining. **History —** H3 main mine adit (with audio-visual presentation; H4 crashed ropeway bucket; H5 'in' (thicker) and 'out' ropes of a 47-tower aerial ropeway (collapsed after five months).

No. 30

Golden Stairs – Ruined Castle

*This Blue Mountains National Park track at
Katoomba offers vistas, forest vegetation
and interesting geological features*

◆ **Length:** 8 or 12½ km (depends on start point)

◆ **Time from CBD**: 2½ hours; rail access (with taxi)

◆ **Duration:** Short day/day

◆ **Children:** 9 years+

◆ **Nearest Refreshment:** Katoomba

◆ **Water:** Scenic Railway tourist complex and picnic area. Carry water

◆ **Toilets:** As for water

◆ **Track:** Signposting; mainly constructed; obvious; some uneven surfaces; some facilities; high use

◆ **Ups 'n' downs:** One steep descent (160 in 800 m); several short, steep ascents and descents

◆ **Start:** There are two possibilities: (a) as for walk 29, for the longer walk; *or* (b) at the Golden Stairs car park about 1¾ km along Glenraphael Dr on Narrow Neck Plateau. Both starting points can be accessed by taxi from Katoomba Station.

TRACK NOTES

◆ If starting from (a), see the notes for the first two stages of walk 29. If starting from (b), locate the steel 'Golden Stairs' signpost and an information board ❶ on the left of Glenraphael Dr.

From here the Golden Stairs Track is followed to the Federal Pass Track ❷. There are spectacular views of the landslides on the opposite cliff face, and note the transition from low to tall eucalypt forest.

◆ Turn south (right) along the Federal Pass Track and proceed to the signpost indicating the Ruined Castle Track ❹. For much of the way you will be passing through temperate rainforest. The ruins at ❸ probably mark the site of a miners' camp.

◆ Make the short, steep climb to the ridge and on to the Ruined Castle 🍎, a collection of boulders and pinnacles resulting from erosion along vertical joint planes and relatively softer shale and claystone strata within the sandstone. The wondrous panorama from the top of the Castle encompasses Mount Solitary (south-east), Castle Head (north-west), Cedar Valley (south) and Jamison Valley (east).

◆ Return to the track junction at the foot of the Golden Stairs. Here there is a choice: (a) return to the Golden Stairs car park via the Stairs; *or* (b) continue on the Federal Pass Track to the Scenic Railway (or Furber Stairs, if feeling energetic) using the notes and map for walk 29.

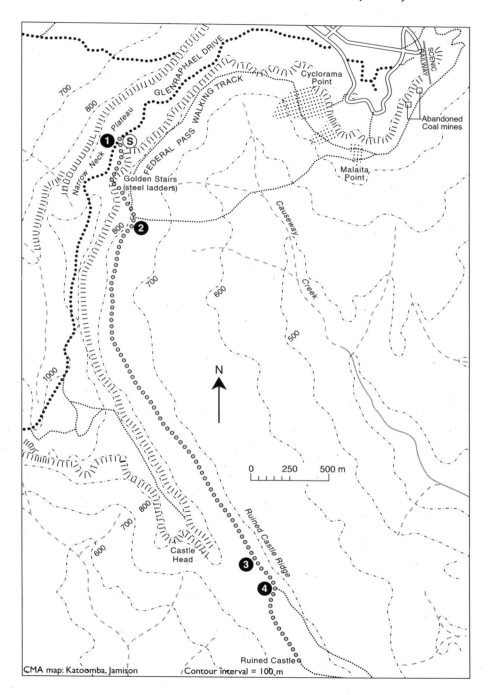

700

800

GLENRAPHAEL DRIVE

FEDERAL PASS WALKING TRACK

Narrow Neck Plateau

Cyclorama Point

Abandoned Coal mines

Malaita Point

1 (S)

Golden Stairs
(steel ladders)

2

800

700

Causeway

Creek

600

500

1000

N

0   250   500 m

800

700

600

Castle Head

Ruined Castle Ridge

3

4

Ruined Castle

CMA map: Katoomba, Jamison   Contour interval = 100 m

No. 31

Braeside Walk – Govetts Leap – Pulpit Rock – Popes Glen

*This walk combines pleasant creek and stunning
cliff-top walking in the Blue Mountains
National Park at Blackheath*

◆ **Length:** 12 km; or omit the Pulpit Rock walk by turning left onto the track through Popes Glen at **5**, 6½ km

◆ **Time from CBD**: 2½ hours; rail access

◆ **Duration:** Short day

◆ **Children:** 9 years+

◆ **Nearest Refreshment:** Blackheath

◆ **Water:** Memorial Park, Govetts Leap; Pulpit Rock. Carry water

◆ **Toilets:** As for water

◆ **Track:** Some signposting; 2½ km constructed; obvious; some uneven surfaces; facilities; moderate–high use

◆ **Ups 'n' downs:** One moderate ascent

and descent (80 in 800 m); several shorter moderate ascents and descents

◆ **Start:** Blackheath Station or Memorial Park, Prince Edward St (see map).

TRACK NOTES

◆ From Memorial Park **1**, proceed up Prince Edward St to Govetts Leap Rd and turn east (left). If you are coming from the railway station, stay in Govetts Leap Rd. Take the next street on the right, Boreas St. At the end, turn east (left) into Braeside St. After about 300 m you will see a fire trail on your right marked by an old sign indicating Braeside Walk and Bridal Veil Falls (Govetts Leap Falls).

Popes Glen

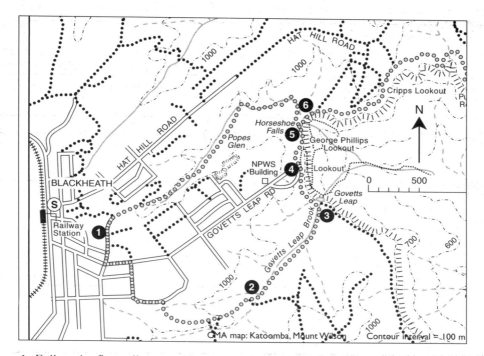

♦ Follow the fire trail to a parking area ❷. A sign indicates the bush track to take to the Govetts Leap Falls. When the Falls are reached, go to the lookout ❸ a few metres to the right for a stunning view of the valley of Govetts Creek, the Govetts Leap Falls, the hanging swamps on the cliff face north of the falls, and Pulpit Rock, the seemingly detached pinnacle.

♦ Cross Govetts Leap Brook and proceed north to Govetts Leap Lookout ❹. This is a superb opportunity to observe the majesty of the sheer, much-jointed and immense cliffs for which the Blue Mountains are famous. The V-shaped hanging valleys etched into the cliffs are easy to identify. The obvious peaks in the distance are the basalt-capped Mount Tomah and Mount Hay. In the forest canopy

below the lookout, note the denser and deeper green foliage, indicating warm-temperate rainforest.

♦ From Govetts Leap Lookout, follow the signposted cliff-top track, past the turn off to Popes Glen ❺ and on to the top of the Horseshoe Falls ❻. Continue on to Pulpit Rock ❼ and a splendid spot for lunch 🍎. On the way, take in more views of the Govetts Leap Falls and the dramatic sandstone walls, punctuated by hanging valleys. The sloping sides of the valley below the vertical cliffs have formed in 260 million year-old Permian marine sediments, outcrops of which may be visible just above the creek.

♦ Return to the turnoff to Popes Glen ❺, and take the track up Popes Glen Creek to Dell St and Memorial Park or the station. *Beware slippery rock surfaces.*

No. 32

Perrys Lookdown – Blue Gum Forest

The outstanding highlights of this challenging walk in the Blue Mountains National Park north of Blackheath are spectacular valley and cliff panoramas, and the famous Blue Gum Forest

- **Length:** 4 km
- **Time from CBD:** 2½ hours; rail access (with taxi)
- **Duration:** Day

- **Children:** 11 years+
- **Nearest Refreshment:** Blackheath
- **Water:** Perrys Lookdown camping area. Carry water

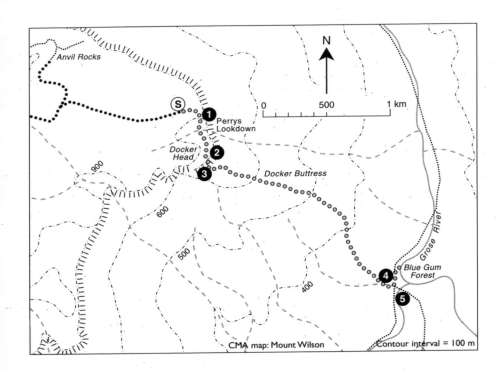

CMA map: Mount Wilson

Contour interval = 100 m

Tall Blue Gum in Blue Gum Forest

- **Toilets:** As for water

- **Track:** Signposting; unconstructed but some development; obvious; some uneven surfaces and many steps; no facilities; low–moderate use

- **Ups 'n' downs:** One very steep descent and ascent (300 in 500 m); one steep/moderate descent and ascent (280 in 1000 m)

- **Start:** Perrys Lookdown camping area and car park off Hat Hill Rd, Blackheath.

TRACK NOTES

This walk involves one continuous, very steep/steep descent and ascent. Attempt it only in dry conditions, and if you are fit.

◆ From the start, the track drops gently to Perrys Lookdown ❶ and then across a gully to Docker Lookout ❷.

The spectacular panorama from ❶ and ❷ takes in the basalt-capped Mount Banks (north) and Mount Hay (east), and the dramatic Grose Valley. The tall, sheer and much-jointed cliffs that enclose the valley are formed mainly from Narrabeen sandstone.

◆ Beyond ❷, the track enters a very steep, narrow gully to emerge half-way down the cliff line ❸. Another steep descent follows to the top of Docker Buttress.

◆ The walk down the buttress is less steep and finally becomes level as Blue Gum Forest is entered. The vegetation in the gully includes Blackwattle and several species of fern. The forest itself consists of huge, old trees of Round-leaved Blue Gum.

◆ From the track junction in Blue Gum Forest ❹ walk directly ahead for 20 m and then take the left-hand fork to Govetts Creek ❺ 🍎, or turn west (left) and follow the track through the forest to find a pleasant picnic spot on the Grose River.

◆ Retrace your steps to ❹ and rejoin the Perrys Lookdown Track for the return walk. Take plenty of rests and use these times to note the wide variety of trees, shrubs and flowers.

No. 33

Porters Pass

This popular track in the Blue Mountains National Park at Blackheath offers valley views, a mix of vegetation communities, rock overhangs and other cliff-line features

- **Length:** 4½ km; or a return trip from the Bundarra St Track head to Centennial Glen via ⑥, 3 km.

- **Time from CBD:** 2½ hours; rail access

- **Duration:** Half day

- **Children:** 9 years+

- **Nearest Refreshment:** Blackheath

- **Water:** Carry water

- **Toilets:** Blackheath Station; in car park behind Ivanhoe Hotel, corner of Govetts Leap Rd and Great Western Hwy

- **Track:** Some signposting; 1½ km constructed (road); obvious; uneven surfaces; no facilities; moderate–high use

- **Ups 'n' downs:** One moderate ascent (190 in 1500 m); one moderate descent (160 in 900 m)

- **Start:** Blackheath Station or, if using car transport, the end of Burton St.

TRACK NOTES

Take special care on sections of this track, especially in winter, when there may be patches of ice.

◆ Take Waragil and Wombat Sts to reach the signposted track head at the end (on right-hand side) of Burton St. Walk down the track, ignoring the track going off to the north (right). After about 20 minutes, an open, heathy area at the top of Porters Pass is reached. Take the side-track on the left to a rocky outcrop ❶ for impressive views, framed by Porters Pass Gully and Shipley Plateau, of Megalong Valley and the Hampton area.

◆ Return to the main track, which descends through the cliff line past attractive clumps of fern on the cliff face at ❷. Before the base of the cliff line is reached, a creek is crossed several times. The medium eucalypt and gully forest here features the very attractive Blue Mountains Ash.

◆ Follow the track to where a short flight of steps brings you to an overhang ❸ 🍎, from which there are more pleasant views. As you make your way up the gully, note the chalk marks and bolts indicating rock climbing activity. Take time to enjoy the views of the swimming holes in Centennial Creek. Among the bird species to be encountered here are the striking Crimson Rosella and King Parrot.

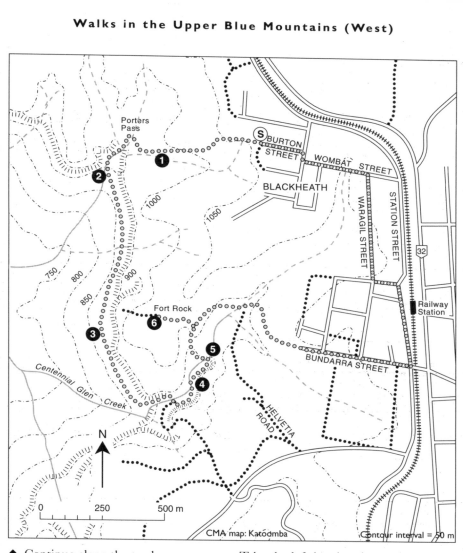

CMA map: Katoomba   Contour interval = 50 m

◆ Continue along the track, across Centennial Glen Creek to steps past a waterfall. Just beyond this point a (dead-end) track goes straight ahead. The track to follow goes up the stairs to the right — marked by an arrow on a tree indicating (incorrectly) 'Porters Pass'. At the top of the short climb, turn north (left) at the track junction.

Take the left-hand option again at the next junction and proceed on past cliffs to more steps and the side-track to Fort Rock ❻ for more attractive views.

◆ Return to the main track and follow it across a small creek and then on to Bundarra St and the short street walk to Blackheath Railway Station.

No. 34

Evans Lookout – Grand Canyon – Neates Glen

Visit a canyon, and enjoy a spectacular panorama and diverse vegetation on this classic walk in the Blue Mountains National Park at Blackheath

♦ **Length:** 7 km; or omit ❸, 6 km; or pick-up at Greaves Ck car park, 6 km

♦ **Time from CBD:** 2½ hours; rail access (taxi required)

♦ **Duration:** Half day

♦ **Children:** 9 years+

♦ **Nearest Refreshment:** Blackheath

♦ **Water:** Evans Lookout; Neates Glen

♦ **Toilets:** Evans Lookout

♦ **Track:** Some signposting; unconstructed; obvious; many irregular steps; facilities; moderate–high usage

♦ **Ups 'n' downs:** One moderate/steep descent (170 in 1100 m) and one steep ascent (160 in 700 m)

♦ **Start:** Evans Lookout at the end of Evans Lookout Rd, Blackheath. If you have only one vehicle, it is suggested that you leave it at the Neates Glen car park, where the walk finishes, and walk from there to the start — a distance of 1.3 km along the Evans Lookout Rd.

TRACK NOTES

♦ The track begins at a flight of stone steps behind Evans Lookout. Initially it follows a spur south to a rocky outcrop

❶ offering a great view of Carne Walls before making a (signposted) turn west (right) and dropping into a gully.

♦ The track follows the gully, staying with the creek for part of the way but

Coral Heath, *Epacris microphylla*

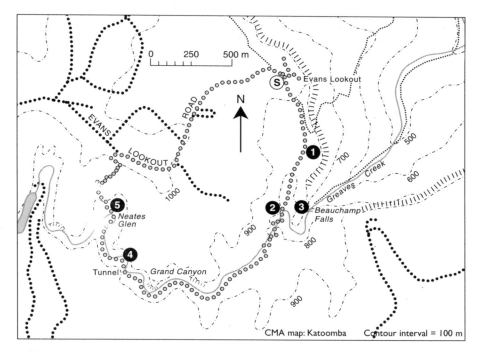

CMA map: Katoomba   Contour interval = 100 m

rising a little away from it towards the bottom of the gully. The vegetation in the gully changes rapidly from low and medium eucalypt forest to patches of warm-temperate rainforest.

◆ Where the gully joins the gorge of Greaves Creek ❷, a track junction is reached. The recommended option is to turn left and to make the 600 m return detour (a descent and an ascent of 80 m are involved) to Beauchamp Falls ❸. Otherwise, turn right and proceed along the track in the direction of Neates Glen.

◆ Initially, the track follows the creek. Near the actual exit of the Grand Canyon, it climbs steeply away from the creek but returns to the very edge of the Grand Canyon. The walk along the edge provides glimpses of the confined and dark depths of the

canyon, and of its steep, water-worn walls where, amazingly, ferns and other vegetation manage to exist.

◆ The track stays with the canyon for some distance, passes behind a small waterfall, climbs gently through a short, natural tunnel and then descends to a rock overhang behind a wide, sandy clearing ❹ ◗ featuring a large stand of Blackwattle.

◆ From ❹, ascend the short flight of stairs and continue on to where the track turns north, crosses Greaves Creek ❺ and enters Neates Glen. The ascent through the pleasant gully forest of the Glen is steep but when it emerges from the gully into more open eucalypt forest the grade becomes progressively more gradual.

◆ Return to Evans Lookout.

No. 35

Megalong Valley Road – Coxs River via the Six Foot Track

Walk through the Megalong Valley south of Blackheath along the historic Six Foot Track through open forest and farmland to the picturesque Coxs River

- ◆ **Length:** 14 km
- ◆ **Time from CBD:** 2½ hours
- ◆ **Duration:** Day
- ◆ **Children:** 11 years+
- ◆ **Nearest Refreshment:** Megalong Valley or Blackheath

- ◆ **Water:** Carry water
- ◆ **Toilets:** Old Ford Reserve; camping area at Coxs River
- ◆ **Track:** Signposting; 12 km unconstructed; obvious; some uneven surfaces and steps; no facilities; low–moderate use

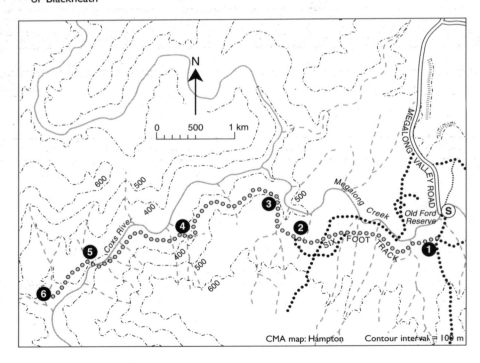

Native bees' nest under rock overhang, Six Foot Track

◆ **Ups 'n' downs:** One steep descent and ascent (60 in 400 m); several shorter steep ascents and descents

◆ **Start:** Junction (signposted) of the Six Foot Track and Megalong Valley Rd, 400 m south of the Old Ford Reserve, Megalong. At Blackheath, cross the railway line and turn immediately left to link up with the Megalong Valley Rd.

TRACK NOTES

The part of the Six Foot Track to Coxs River goes off to the west. The track is indicated throughout its length by signs and red-and-white Department of Land and Water Conservation markers. *Only the route indicated by these markers should be used.* Note the Old Megalong Cemetery ❶ near the start.

◆ Proceed on the track, through farmland initially and then through bushland to the Coxs River.

◆ At ❷ enjoy views of the sandstone cliffs of Narrow Neck Plateau (east), Gibraltar Walls (south-west), and Gibraltar Sugarloaf, the granite, dome-shaped hill rising from the Coxs River valley (west). At ❸, observe how the Coxs River has carved a 'valley in a valley'. Along the track from ❸ to the river are reminders that the track was originally constructed in 1884–85 as a bridle trail linking Katoomba and Jenolan Caves (a Department of Lands brochure gives more details). Look for nests of native bees in the small overhang at ❹.

◆ Continue on through a fringing forest dominated by River She-oak to the suspension bridge ❺. You can stop here for lunch 🍴 or cross the bridge and proceed to the large camping area at ❻.

◆ Return the same way.

No. 36

Little Zig Zag – Rienits Pass

This walk in the Blue Mountains National Park at Mount Victoria follows an interesting and historic track and features panoramas, an impressive sandstone cave, and handsome forests

◆ **Length:** 5 km; or from Start to ❷ return (1.4 km)

◆ **Time from CBD:** 2½ hours; rail access

◆ **Duration:** Short day

◆ **Children:** 9 years+

◆ **Nearest Refreshment:** Mount Victoria

◆ **Water:** Mount Victoria Station. Carry water

◆ **Toilets:** As for water

◆ **Track:** Some signposting; 2½ km unconstructed; obvious; some uneven surfaces and steps; no facilities; low–moderate use

◆ **Ups 'n' downs:** One steep/very steep ascent (230 in 1200 m); one steep descent (200 in 700 m)

◆ **Start:** End of Kanimbla Valley Rd (Innes Rd), Mount Victoria. Cars are best left at the junction of Hooper and Carlisle Sts.

TRACK NOTES

◆ Fifty metres from the start, take the short side-track to Pulpit Rock ❶ to take in views of the Kanimbla and Megalong valleys, Gibraltar Rocks and Gibraltar Sugarloaf, a dome-shaped granite outcrop. Return to the main track and follow it to where it turns south (left) to become the first 'zig' of the Little Zig Zag. Avoid the track along the telephone line. Look for pick marks in rock just before the first hairpin bend. Proceed down the Zig Zag, noting the skilfully made embankments, fine, 100-year-old examples of hand-crafted stonemasonry.

◆ Continue on, passing, at the sixth bend, the junction with the North Track. A sign 'Cave' at the seventh bend marks the short but very uneven side-track to the Bushrangers Cave ❷. The white squares and markings on the cliff face indicate rock climbing routes.

◆ Return to the track and continue the zig-zag descent. A blue marker and a faded sign 'sugarloaf' on a rock indicate sidetracks to be ignored. When the track reaches the first flat, grassy, open woodland area, a Y-junction ❸ will be encountered. Take the Rienits Pass Track to the east (left). A broken sign 'Renitz' might be in place at the foot of a tree. The track winds off the ridge and passes through a tall eucalypt forest featuring Blue Mountains Ash and Blue Mountains Stringybark. It becomes level for a short stretch before climbing

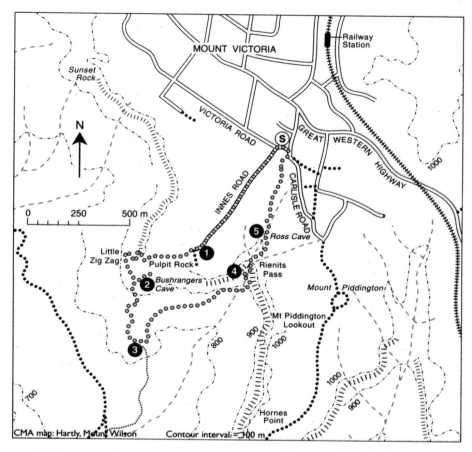

steadily, but steeply in places, towards the base of the cliffs.

♦ The track stays on the western (left-hand) side of the creek (any track appearing to go right towards the creek, should be ignored) until it passes close (40 m) to the cliffs and waterfall at the top of the valley. Here, the track crosses the creek and climbs steeply again to the base of the cliffs where it turns left. (The short sidetrack to the right leads to a pleasant waterfall♦)

♦ Follow the track under the cliffs, through Wilsons Glen ❹, past a yellow sign (Ross Cave/Wilson Glen) and up though a narrow gully to the cliff top.

♦ Beyond the top of the narrow gully, the track crosses the creek just before a junction with a track coming in from the right. Ignore this track but continue up the creek. Watch for the sign indicating Ross Cave ❺. About 400 m past the cave, a T-junction and fence are reached. Turn right and proceed to Carlisle Parade for the walk to the station or your car.

No. 37

Mount Banks – Banks Wall

*Highlights of this Blue Mountains National Park walk
near Bell include stunning panoramas and
various vegetation communities*

- **Length:** 11 km; or walk the road to **8**, 11 km; or turn left at **5**, 4½km

- **Time from CBD:** 2½ hours

- **Duration:** Short day

- **Children:** 9 years+

- **Nearest Refreshment:** Bilpin, Mount Victoria

- **Water:** Mount Banks picnic area; Banks Walls. Carry water

- **Toilets:** Mount Banks picnic area

- **Track:** Some signposting; 2 km unconstructed; obvious; some uneven surfaces; some facilities; moderate–high use

- **Ups 'n' downs:** One moderate/steep ascent (180 in 1000 m); one moderate/steep descent (170 in 1000 m); several short, moderate ascents and descents

- **Start:** Mount Banks picnic area, located 1 km south from a signposted turn-off on Bells Line of Road (47 km from Hawkesbury River Bridge at North Richmond; 11 km from road junction at Bell). From the signpost, follow the gravel road.

TRACK NOTES

- From the NPWS Track sign **1** near the locked gate located west (right) of the picnic area, take the walking track (marked by a small walking track symbol). Follow this track, past the clump of Blue Mountains Mallee and across the very exposed heathland, in which stunted Drumsticks (that turn rust-coloured in colder weather) and Dagger Hakea are prominent. Ignore the lesser track going off to the east (left) just before a prominent rock outcrop **2** is reached.

- Continue up the track, *which can be slippery in places*, noting the change in vegetation from heath to medium/ tall eucalypt forest. Initially, the dominant trees are Silver-Top Ash but these are replaced by Brown Barrel nearer the crown of the mountain where the red-brown colour of the soil indicates its basaltic origin. The richer basalt soil also supports an abundance of Bracken and Rasp Fern.

- As the top is approached, note a track going off to the east (left). The cairn of fine-grained basalt rock marking the top of the mountain is 40 m beyond this junction. Go 50 m directly beyond the cairn to a point **3**

Walks in the Upper Blue Mountains (West)

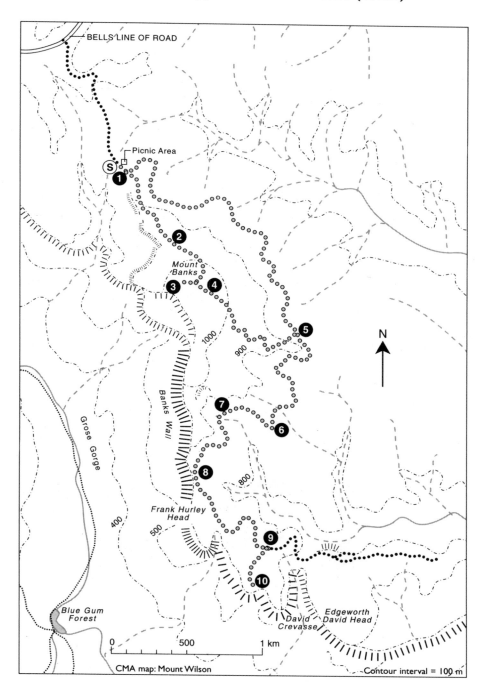

BELLS LINE OF ROAD

Picnic Area

(S) ①

②

Mount Banks

③ ④

1000

⑤

900

Banks Wall

⑦ ⑥

800

⑧

Frank Hurley Head

400

500

⑨

Grose Gorge

⑩

Blue Gum Forest

David Crevasse

Edgeworth David Head

N

0   500   1 km

CMA map: Mount Wilson

Contour interval = 100 m

providing views of Mount Victoria, Blackheath and Blue Gum Forest (in the valley).

◆ From the cairn, retrace your steps 40 m and take the track to the east (now on your right). Follow this track for about 100 m south-east down the slope until a weather-worn picnic table and fireplace are reached ❹. ❧ This is a good place for an eating stop. To the right of the table, traces of a four-wheel-drive track will be found. Follow this track to its junction ❺ with the Banks Walls Rd. There will be glimpses on the way of Mount Hay, the cliffs of the Grose Valley and the distant Sydney skyline.

◆ At the road junction turn south (right) and follow the road to Banks Walls ❽. Note the termite mound at ❻ and the interestingly patterned iron banding in the rock at ❼. The vegetation along the track includes patches of medium eucalypt forest and, in early summer, look out for Waratah and Christmas Bush. From Banks Walls, follow the road for 1 km to where a very obvious track ❾ goes off to the south-west (right). This track will take you to a spectacular viewing point ❿.❧

◆ Return to the picnic area by staying on the Mount Banks Track; that is, go straight on at the track junction ❺.

Coal mine adit

Glow Worm Tunnel – Old Coach Road – Pagoda Track

This spectacular walk in the Wollemi National Park north of Lithgow follows an abandoned railway line through a tunnel and under majestic cliffs

◆ **Length:** 10 km; or return from "The Bluffs" through the tunnel or along Bells Grotto Track to the main track, 5½ km

◆ **Time from CBD:** 3½ hours

◆ **Duration:** Day

◆ **Children:** 9 years+

◆ **Nearest Refreshment:** Lithgow

◆ **Water:** Bungleboori Picnic Area (on access road). Carry water

◆ **Toilets:** At start of walk

◆ **Track:** Some signposting; all constructed; obvious; some uneven surfaces; no facilities; moderate–high use

◆ **Ups 'n' downs:** One moderate ascent (110 in 1600 m)

◆ **Start:** Terminus of the Glow Worm Tunnel Rd, 36 km from Lithgow. At the eastern end of Main St, Lithgow, turn left over the railway and immediately right into Inch St, which is followed for 1.3 km to where a sign 'Glow Worm Tunnel' indicates a left turn into Tourist Dr #1. Follow the Drive markers to the start of the walk, taking the right-hand fork at Bungleboori Picnic Area and at the turn-off to the Youth Insearch Centre. As you proceed, take note of the cuttings,

embankments and tunnel, now occupied by the road, but originally constructed for the Wolgan Valley railway line.

TRACK NOTES

Take a reliable torch for the safe negotiation of Glow Worm Tunnel.

◆ Follow the track along the route of the railway to, and through, the Glow Worm Tunnel. The surrounding tall eucalypt forest contains many fine specimens of Blue Mountains Ash. The cutting at ❶, just past the washed-away section of railway embankment, is located in a natural split or joint in the rock. The glow worms, larvae of the fungus gnat, can be seen on the roof and walls of the darkest section of the tunnel.

◆ After walking through the tunnel, detour left immediately to visit Bells Grotto ❷ and the overhangs 150 m beyond. The massive tree that is passed is a specimen of Blue Mountains Ash. The source of the orange precipitate in the water is iron in the sandstone of the area and is the product of bacterial activity. Note the iron banding in the wall of the second overhang.

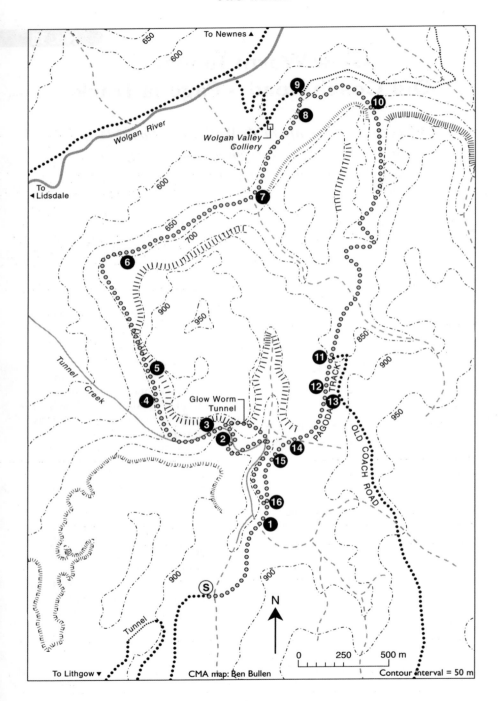

To Newnes ▲

650

600

Wolgan River

To
◄ Lidsdale

600

650

700

9

8

Wolgan Valley
Colliery

10

7

6

900

950

Tunnel Creek

5

4

11

850

900

12

950

13

Glow Worm
Tunnel

3

2

14

PAGODA TRACK

OLD COACH ROAD

15

16

1

900

900

S

Tunnel

N

0   250   500 m

To Lithgow ▼

CMA map: Ben Bullen

Contour interval = 50 m

Along the Old Coach Road

◆ Return to the main track and follow it through 'Penrose' Gorge, under the cliffs ('The Bluffs') and on to ❻ 🥾. Both Soft and Rough Tree ferns will be encountered in the gorge. At ❸ are the concrete remains of a small dam that formerly provided water for the locomotives working the line. Look for the concrete skirting under the rock face at ❹, probably placed to prevent rock falls by retarding the erosion of the softer underlying claystone. Other examples and legacies of railway engineering along this section of the track include embankments, stone culverts, steel spikes in the cliff face at ❺ and the stone-lined cutting at ❻. The view to the west is of Wolgan Valley and Donkey Mountain.

◆ Continue on to where the track meets the Old Coach Rd ❾, passing on the way a coal mine adit ❼ (dangerous to enter) and an interesting sandstone cave at ❽. Grey Gum is prominent in the medium eucalypt forest that lines the track.

◆ Turn right at the junction ❾ and make the steady climb up the Old Coach Rd to the end of the Pagoda Track ⓫, taking care to note the fine rock embankment at ❿.

◆ From ⓫, proceed south (right) up the Pagoda Track for about 150 m. Take the indistinct track to the right for about 30 m before walking left to the large, weathered rock ⓬, where there are the remains of what was probably an explosives store.

◆ Return to Pagoda Track and climb the final 50 m to the saddle. After detouring left to look at the remains of a ropeway or slide from the Old Coach Rd at ⓭, follow the track to where it crosses the watercourse. Here, walk (right) down the watercourse for 25 m to examine the remains of a well just off to the right ⓮.

◆ Back on the track, continue south, past an area ⓯ where the builders of the railway line had their camp for a time, to the junction ⓰ with Glow Worm Tunnel Track and on to the parking area.

No. 39

Wollangambe Track

*Highlights of this relatively demanding walk in
the Wollemi National Park at Mount Wilson
include an impressive forest, and
wilderness and canyon scenery*

♦ **Length:** 8 km; or return from ❹, 5 km

♦ **Time from CBD:** 2 hours

♦ **Duration:** Day

♦ **Children:** 11 years+

♦ **Nearest Refreshment:** Mount Victoria,
Bilpin

♦ **Water:** Carry water

♦ **Toilet:** Founders Corner at the intersection of The Avenue and Mount Irvine Rd,
Mount Wilson

♦ **Track:** No signposting (beyond the
start); 6½ km unconstructed; obvious;
many uneven surfaces; no facilities;
moderate–high use

♦ **Ups 'n' downs:** This walk consists
entirely of two moderate/steep descents
and ascents (300 in 3000 m, 70 in 500 m)

♦ **Start:** Wollangambe Track car park ❶
adjacent to the Rural Fire Brigade building, Mount Wilson.

TRACK NOTES

*Don't do this walk in very hot (30°C plus)
weather.*

♦ From ❶, follow the track south-east
past the information board (with its
cautionary message for the unprepared)
to a T-junction. Turn south (left) and
proceed to where another T-intersec-
tion is visible about 40 to 50 m ahead.
Locate a narrower track ❷ going off to
the south-east (right) and follow it
across a fire trail and into a tall eucalypt
forest featuring Manna Gum, Blue
Mountains Stringybark, Brown Barrel,
tree fern (Rough and Soft) and a
ground-fern understorey. Note the transition from 'softer' vegetation (e.g.
Lomatia siliafolia, Cassinia aureonitens) to
sclerophyllous flora (e.g. Tea-tree,
Geebung, Flannel-flower, banksias,
drumsticks) as the red-brown basalt soil
thins and gives way to sandy soil.

♦ As you continue down the track,
note the rock outcrop where the track is
formed of six or so natural steps. A little
farther on you will pass a larger outcrop
on the left and, shortly after, another on
the right. At the next outcrop ❸, there
is a track junction. One track (indicated
by a faint curved arrow on the rock at
your feet) goes west (left) round and
through a gap in the rock; the other
track goes straight ahead (north).

Walks in the Upper Blue Mountains (West)

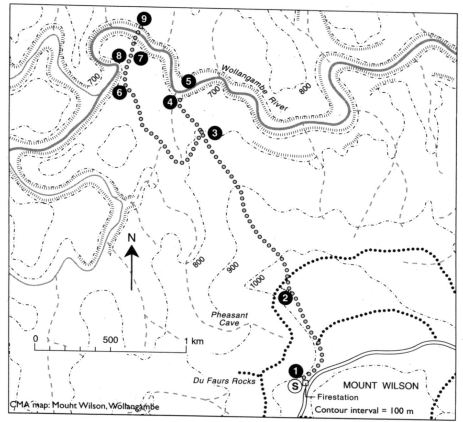

◆ Take the track straight ahead and follow it to another rock outcrop at the top of a short, steep gully leading into the gorge of the Wollangambe River. Make your way across the outcrop to the edge of the gorge ❹ 🍎 for a view down the Wollangambe Canyon ❺ with its precipitous walls and long tranquil pools. Note how the gully forest in the gorge contrasts sharply with the low eucalypt, predominantly Scribbly Gum, forest on the cliffs tops and slopes above. Ignore tracks going off in a westerly direction (left), possibly marked by small cairns.

◆ Return to the junction ❸ and take the track which goes round and through the rock. Follow this track until the Wollangambe Gorge is again in view. The viewpoint at ❻ should be visited in order to view the impressive gorge of Bells Creek.

◆ After making the short, steep descent to the saddle at ❼, you have two options. The first is to go to the excellent picnic, but not swimming, spot at ❽ 🍎. The second is to take the rougher, northerly track to ❾ 🍎. Here a swim of sorts is possible.

137

*The trackless river walk from ❾ to the start of Wollangambe Canyon ❺ is not difficult when the **shallowest** water at this point is ankle-deep. However, once under way, you will need to be wearing swimwear and light protective footwear, be ready to negotiate fallen timber and undertake a couple of chest-deep wades. Swim in the canyon itself*

only if you are a very strong, confident swimmer and if you are not alone. Fatigue, chilling and cramping can occur quickly in the cold water of the canyons, even on the hottest of summer days.

◆ Return to the start by the same route.

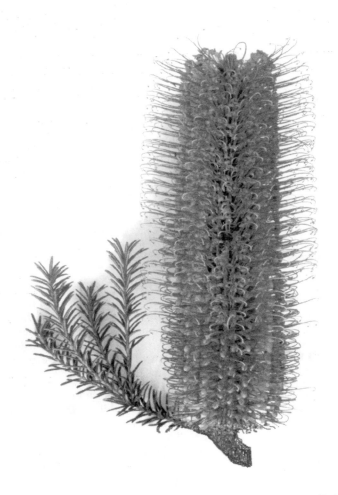

Heath Banksia, *Banksia ericifolia*

Walks in the Southern Blue Mountains/Illawarra Plateau (South-west and South)

Although there are only five of them, the walks in this group are extraordinarily diverse. Walk 40, the most 'far-flung' of the walks, has exceptional attractions including vast panoramas, views of the Kanangra 'Deep' and the Kowmung Valley, and a range of interesting geological features. Walk 41 offers spectacular valley views as well as the charm of a delightful stretch of the Nattai River. Walk 44 combines a different experience of the Nattai River with an opportunity to travel an abandoned railway line. Although smaller in scale than that of the Nattai, the valley visited in walk 42 has beautiful forest vegetation and interesting bird life. Walk 43 provides an opportunity to see rare bird species as well as to enjoy the rainforest and heathland vegetation and spectacular coastal views from the Illawarra Escarpment. Panoramas and diverse types of vegetation are also features of walk 45.

No. 40

Kanangra Walls – Cottage Rock

*South of the Jenolan Caves in the Blue Mountains
National Park, this walk offers stunning
panoramas and dramatic landforms*

◆ **Length:** 9 km; or return from ❸, 2 km

◆ **Time from CBD:** 4 hours

◆ **Duration:** Short day (shorter/easier option)

◆ **Children:** 9 years+

◆ **Nearest Refreshment:** Jenolan Caves

◆ **Water:** Jenolan Caves. Carry water

◆ **Toilets:** Jenolan Caves; Kanangra Walls car park

◆ **Track:** Some signposting; mainly unconstructed; obvious (except across rock); some uneven surfaces; high steps and mud; no facilities; low–moderate use

◆ **Ups 'n' downs:** One steep descent and ascent (50 in 150 m); several shorter moderate/steep ascents and descents

◆ **Start:** Kanangra Walls car park at the end of the Kanangra Walls Rd, which leaves the Jenolan Caves/Oberon Rd about 3 km west of Jenolan Caves.

TRACK NOTES

The final part of the ascent of Cottage Rock involves a scramble, which less agile or able-bodied adults and children younger than 12 years of age might not be able to manage, even with assistance.

◆ Go to the end of the road and take the marked footpath. Turn east (right) at the first junction (or go straight on for 50 m to a lookout and then return). The magnificent panorama from the lookout encompasses Mount Cloudmaker and Kanangra Walls. The structure of the Walls is particularly interesting geologically. Note how the horizontal sandstones of the Sydney basin overlie older, tilted and folded Late Devonian sedimentary rocks. Follow the track into the gully, detouring 30 m south (right) past a remarkable outcrop of 270-280 million year-old conglomerate rock to view the Dance Floor Cave ❷, which was a dance venue a century ago.

◆ Return to the main track and turn east (right) and proceed up the steps and across the plateau area known as Seymour Top. The track, which stays within 20 to 30 m of the cliff edge, might not be clear on rocky patches, but it is obvious through the vegetation. About 1 km (20 to 30 mins) from the start, the track descends slightly and crosses a narrow stretch of plateau. Where the plateau widens again, the track begins to ascend and passes close to the cliff edge ❸. The much photographed views from here are of

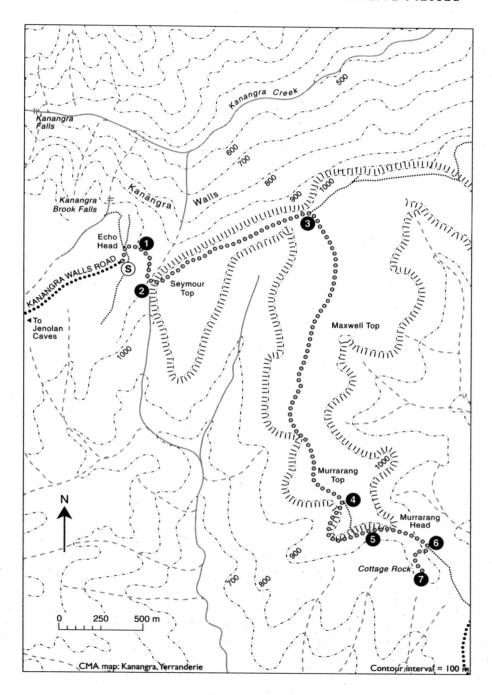

CMA map: Kanangra, Yerranderie

Contour interval = 100 m

the 550 m trench of Kanangra Deep, Kanangra Falls, Kanangra Brook Falls and, directly across the valley, Thurat Spires, which were probably part of the ancient shoreline of the Sydney Basin.

◆ From ❸, follow the track as it swings south (right) *away from the cliff line*. Ignore the track going north-east, parallel to the cliff line. Continue walking for about 2 km through dense heath vegetation, ignoring a side-track leading off to the east (left). Try to use the main track rather than side-tracks to protect the vegetation and restrict erosion damage.

◆ About 2 km (or 30 to 40 minutes) from ❸, look out for a track junction ❹. Both tracks take you to Cottage Rock, but the one going south-east (right) is recommended. Follow it to the Coal Seam Cave ❺ 🍎. The coal outcropping in the cave is part of the same coal measures that occur at Wollongong and Newcastle. Soon after the cave, the track descends steeply to a saddle ❻. Where the track begins to descend around the left-hand side of the ridge, look for a faint track on the right, going up the slope. Follow this track to the summit of the hill and Cottage Rock ❼ for stunning views of the Kowmung River valley, Mount Colong and Mount Cloudmaker.

◆ Return by the same route.

Old Man Banksia, *Banksia serrata*

Starlight's Trail

*Highlights of this walk in Nattai National Park west of
Hilltop include a mix of vegetation communities, and
views of a beautiful river valley and high cliffs*

◆ **Length:** 13 km

◆ **Time from CBD:** 2 hours

◆ **Duration:** Day

◆ **Children:** 9 years+

◆ **Nearest Refreshment:** Thirlmere,
Picton

◆ **Water:** Picton. Carry water

◆ **Toilets:** As for water

◆ **Track:** Some signposting; mainly unconstructed; obvious; some uneven, steep
and gravelly surfaces; no facilities; low–
moderate usage

◆ **Ups 'n' downs:** One moderate/steep
(180 in 1200 m) and three moderate (90
in 1500, 100 in 700, 60 in 500 m)
descents and ascents

◆ **Start:** Entrance to Nattai National Park
west of Hilltop. From Picton, take the
road through Thirlmere (crossing the rail
line) and continue west on the road that
runs next to the line. About 3 km past
the village of Balmoral, the road crosses a
deep rail cutting. Turn right onto a dirt
road 200 m past the cutting. After crossing the rail line, fork left and then turn
sharp right (at a short sealed section)

onto Wattle Ridge Rd. Follow this road
for 6 km to the parking area near the
Park entrance.

TRACK NOTES

◆ From the car park **❶**, follow the road
beyond the gate, round the head of a
gully and then west past a pluviometer
(rain gauge) to a road junction **❷** at the
top of a rise. Turn left at this junction
onto the signposted 'Starlight's Trail'
and follow the road (of sorts) south and
then west for another 500 m to a defi-
nite clearing **❸**.

◆ From the clearing, the road swings
sharply south (left) and begins to rise. A
level foot-track branches to the north
from here also. *Take neither of these*, but
follow a path running initially south-
west from the clearing and marked by a
small cairn of stones. This is Starlight's
Trail and it immediately commences a
steady descent through low eucalypt
forest in which sclerophyllous species
such as banksias, geebungs and erioste-
mons abound.

◆ After another 1 km, the track passes
a rock in which a large cavity has been
eroded **❹** (hence 'toothache rock'),

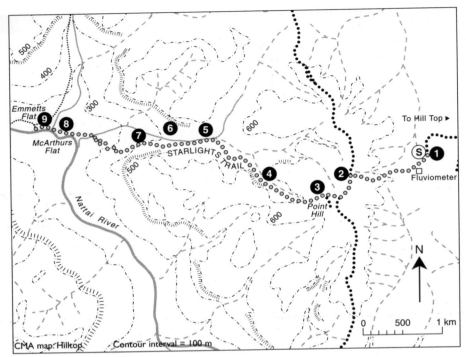

CMA map: Hilltop   Contour interval = 100 m

then continues to descend steadily, joining a creek ⑤. A marked change to the tall eucalypt forest will be apparent.

◆ A few hundred metres farther on, the track is again above the creek and begins to provide views of the Nattai Valley ⑦, with its vertical Hawkesbury Sandstone cliffs and hanging valleys above and more gentle slopes of Permian sediments below. It may be possible to make out cliffs of volcanic rock in the bottom of the gully at ⑥.

◆ From ⑥, the track begins to descend into the valley. *The zig-zag section of the descent is steep, so take care.* When the valley floor is reached, the track crosses a small creek and enters McArthurs Flat ⑧ 🍎. The vegetation around the flat is mainly tall eucalypt forest

containing River Peppermint, Manna Gum, River She-oak, Black Wattle and other acacias. Look out for evidence of former human occupancy of the area.

◆ Pleasant options for exploring the area by the river include taking a closer look at the river itself. Walking downstream (west) for 500 m brings you to Emmetts Flat ⑨ and the remains of a hut (illegally built).

◆ Return to the start by the same route.

The road leaving Emmetts Flat joins the Wattle Ridge Rd and provides a return route to the start. However, attempt this round-trip option only if you are an experienced and fit walker and there is at least six hours of daylight left.

Blue Gum Creek – Little River

*Located in Thirlmere Lakes National Park
near Picton, this walk passes through a
beautiful forest and provides access
to a pleasant stretch of river*

♦ **Length:** 16 km

♦ **Time from CBD:** 1½ hours

♦ **Duration:** Long day

♦ **Children:** 11 years+

♦ **Nearest Refreshment:** Picton, Thirlmere

♦ **Water:** Toilets at Thirlmere Lakes National Park picnic areas. Carry water

♦ **Toilets:** As for water

♦ **Track:** No signposting; constructed; obvious; excellent surface except for loose stones and gravel on some short steep pinches; no facilities; low usage

♦ **Ups 'n' downs:** Mostly level; one moderate steep ascent and descent (40 in 300 m); several short moderate ascents and descents

♦ **Start:** Locked gate on fire road west of Thirlmere Lakes. Cross the railway at Thirlmere, turn left at the roundabout and follow Mittagong Rd for 2.3 km. Turn right into Slades Rd, which takes you into the National Park. Proceed around the lakes and beyond for a distance of about 6 km from the Park entrance. As soon as you see a gate across the road, look for a parking spot.

TRACK NOTES

The walk traverses a catchment area that is jointly administered by Sydney Water and the NPWS. Entry by walkers is permitted but access restrictions apply beyond Little River.

♦ From the locked gate ❶ the road follows the valley of Blue Gum Creek. Under the cliffs of Mount Rice ❷ it turns sharply west and then, after a farther 1 km, almost due north. A feature of this area are fine specimens of Round-leafed Blue Gum with their smooth, shaft-like trunks 30 to 40 m tall. Coachwood, Cedar Wattle, Dwarf Plum-pine, Native Grape are other common species. Bell Miners have colonised parts of the forest.

♦ The road continues on straight and fairly level while the creek begins to drop as the valley narrows. Where the Hawkesbury Sandstone cliffs of Perrott Bluff ❸ loom above, the road curves round a spur and drops to the level of the creek, where the moister environment supports Grey Myrtle and Prickly-leafed Paperbark. Be on the lookout for Crimson Rosellas and Black Cockatoos. It is also possible that Lace Monitors (Goannas) will be about.

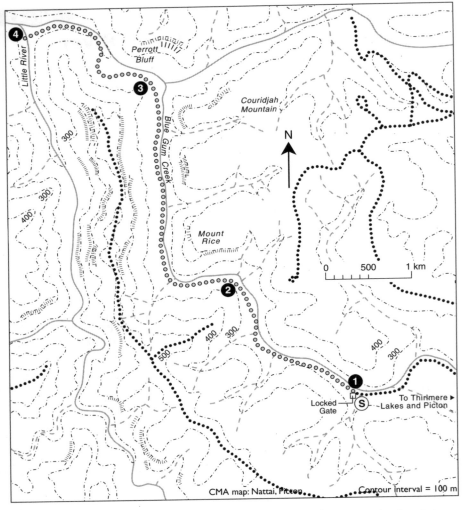

CMA map: Nattai, Picton   Contour interval = 100 m

◆ The track climbs steeply up the hill-side for 300 m and, after skirting several gullies, descends as steeply almost to creek level. After following the creek for another kilometre, the road reaches a picturesque ford **4** on Little River about 200 m upstream from where the river is joined by Blue Gum Creek. The vegetation bordering the river includes River She-oak, Water Gum and Coachwood.

◆ There are good lunch and swimming spots just above the ford 🍎. Return by the same route, allowing at least 2½ hours of daylight.

Barren Grounds Nature Reserve – Griffiths Trail

As well as offering impressive coastal panoramas, this walk near Jamberoo, inland from Kiama, is famed for its heath vegetation and bird life

- **Length:** 8 km
- **Time from CBD:** 2 hours
- **Duration:** Half day
- **Children:** 9 years+
- **Nearest Refreshment:** Jamberoo
- **Water:** Barren Grounds Nature Reserve. Carry water
- **Toilets:** As for water
- **Track:** Signposting; unconstructed but developed, even surface, although muddy and eroded in places; obvious; some facilities; moderate–high usage
- **Ups 'n' downs:** Mainly level
- **Start:** Barren Grounds Nature Reserve picnic area. From Jamberoo take the road towards Albion Park. Turn left into Jamberoo Pass Rd about 1 km out of town. Continue past the Minnamurra Falls turn-off on the right and on to the signposted road turning off left to the Barren Grounds Nature Reserve. (The Royal Australian Ornithological Union visitor centre is passed and might be open.) The Griffiths Trail begins from the picnic area, just below the entrance road. From the Illawarra Hwy, access the start by turning south 2 km east of Robertson.

TRACK NOTES

◆ This walk consists of the Griffiths Trail, a circular walk, combined with a 1 km nature trail through swamp vegetation and warm-temperate rainforest. To take in the nature trail early in the walk, follow the Griffiths Trail northeast from the picnic area. After about 300 m, the nature trail branches off to the north (left). The walk around this trail brings you back to the main track.

◆ When the main track is regained, turn east (left) and visit the Illawarra Lookout ❶ before continuing along the escarpment. Note how the steep cliff in the Hawkesbury Sandstone immediately below the lookout gives way to a more benched slope in the underlying Illawarra Coal Measures. In late winter and spring, the wildflower display in the heath behind the escarpment includes some beautiful but uncommon species such as *Boronia thujona*, *Phebalium diosmeum*, and *Bossiaea kiamensis*. The heath is home also to the rare Eastern Bristlebird (about the size of a Common Mynah, with rich brown and grey colouring) and the Ground Parrot (bright green with yellow or black bars and spots).

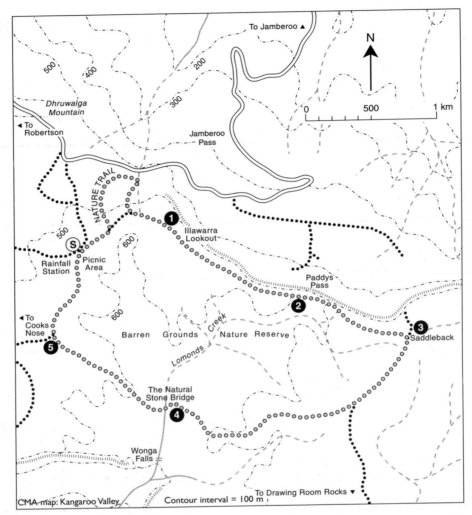

CMA map: Kangaroo Valley   Contour interval = 100 m

◆ After passing through heathland on the escarpment, the track drops into narrow gully ❷ ,which is being 'invaded' by the escarpment as the latter advances south (a nice example of stream capture). Many of the tall forest trees seen on this section of the track are the rare *Eucalyptus dendromorpha* (a mallee in some places but here a tall tree). The track then ascends to a track junction at Saddleback Trig ❸. From here, there are pleasant views across heathland to the low summit of Mount Noorinan and farther away Saddleback Mountain, a volcanic outlier of the escarpment. The track to the north (left) goes about 300 m downhill to another lookout.

♦ Take the right (south) branch at ❸ and proceed to the 'Natural Stone Bridge' at Lomonds Creek ❹ 🍎, where rock-scoured potholes can be seen.

♦ From ❹, the track climbs gradually for the next 1 km (through alternating belts of low open forest and tall heath, wet and boggy in places) to the junction ❺ with the fire trail to Cooks Nose. Take the right turn for the 1 km walk back to the Picnic Area.

Optional extension: The return trip of 5 km from ❺ to Cooks Nose provides attractive views of the farmland and rainforest in Kangaroo Valley. Proceed west from ❺ and at the first and only track junction, turn south (left).

Woody Pear, *Xylomelum pyriforme*

No. 44

Box Vale Railway – Forty Foot Falls

*Explore the route of an abandoned railway
and a scenic riverside track near Mittagong*

◆ **Length:** 10 km; or Box Vale Track return trip, 8 km; or with a side-trip to Forty Foot Falls, 11 km

◆ **Time from CBD:** 2 hours

◆ **Duration:** Short day

◆ **Children:** 9 years+

◆ **Nearest Refreshment:** Mittagong

◆ **Water:** Track head. Carry water

◆ **Toilets:** As for water

◆ **Track:** Some signposting; 3½ km unconstructed; obvious; some uneven surfaces and river crossing on rocks; some facilities; low–moderate use

◆ **Ups 'n' downs:** One steep ascent (110 in 500 m); one steep descent (150 in 600 m)

◆ **Start:** At the Box Vale Track parking area off Box Vale Rd, 3½ km west of Mittagong Post Office. From Mittagong, take the Old Hume Hwy and 100 m past the bridge over the F5 freeway, turn right into Box Vale Rd and then left to the parking area.

TRACK NOTES

◆ From the car park (see information board), follow the signs indicating the Box Vale Track. After crossing Nattai Creek, you will soon be walking on the route of the dismantled Box Vale rail line (opened 1888). Ignore the fire trail that criss-crosses the track.

◆ About 100 m past Casuarina Cutting ❶, note the fire trail going off to the north-west (right) ❷.

Unless you choose the shorter option (a), you will use this trail for the return journey.

◆ Proceed across the ford at Kells Creek ❸, where there once was a trestle bridge, and on through Boulder Cutting ❹, Fern Cutting ❺, aptly named because of its Rough Tree Ferns, and an unlined (indicating stable rock) tunnel ❻ to the signposted picnic area ❼ at the end of the line. A track off to the east (right) takes you to a lookout ❽ for views of Nattai River valley. The many open forest bird species in the area include Crimson Rosella, Golden Rufus Whistler, Grey Thrush and Gang Gang Cockatoo.

◆ Return to the picnic area and follow the track to the north-west (left), shown by yellow markers on trees. The track drops away sharply and becomes broken and loose as it descends a very steep incline.

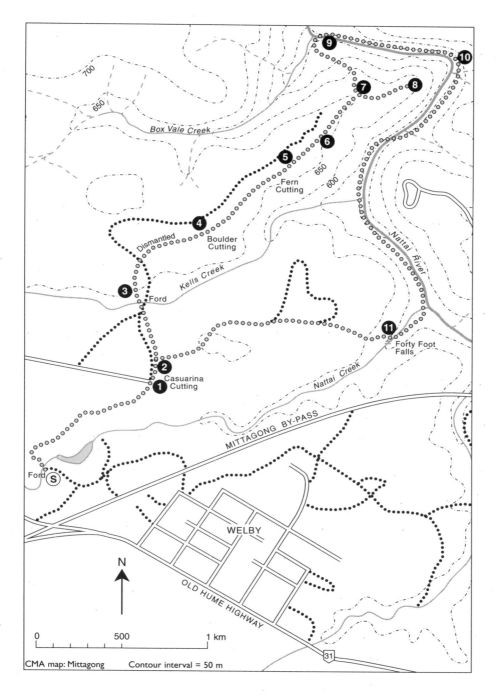

700

650

Box Vale Creek

9

10

7

8

6

5

Fern
Cutting

650

600

4

Dismantled

Boulder
Cutting

Kells Creek

Nattai River

3

Ford

11

Forty Foot
Falls

2

Nattai Creek

1

Casuarina
Cutting

MITTAGONG BY-PASS

Ford **S**

N

WELBY

OLD HUME HIGHWAY

31

| 0 | 500 | 1 km |

CMA map: Mittagong   Contour interval = 50 m

Caution and care are always needed in this section; use the steel cable for support.

From the base of the incline the track goes north-east (right) along Box Vale Creek to the Nattai River **❾🍎**.

◆ Cross the river (on rock) at the Box Vale Creek junction and take the track east (right) upstream. The blue markers indicate the route of the Barrallier Walk from Katoomba to Mittagong.

Be prepared to negotiate fallen trees and flood debris in this section.

Debris in the vegetation along the bank indicates levels of recent 'floods'. Along the way you will pass through a natural sandstone arch **❿**. About 500 m beyond the arch the track crosses the river again (on rock) and stays on the western side, crossing Kells Creek. At the Nattai Creek junction, turn south-west (right) at the signpost and use the yellow markers to follow the track to the Forty Foot Falls. Do not miss the cave behind the falls.

◆ From the Falls, climb the track with its many steps to the fire trail, which takes you to the Box Vale Track for the return trip to the car park.

Tunnel on Box Vale railway

McPhails Fire Trail

Enjoy beautiful forest vegetation and delightful panoramas in the Morton National Park near Kangaroo Valley

♦ **Length:** 18 km; or from Start to ❸ return, 6 km

♦ **Time from CBD:** 2½ hours

♦ **Duration:** Day

♦ **Children:** 11 years+

♦ **Nearest Refreshment:** Kangaroo Valley

♦ **Water:** Carry water

♦ **Toilets:** Bendeela picnic area

♦ **Track:** Some signposting; 2½ km unconstructed; obvious; some uneven surfaces; no facilities; low–moderate use

♦ **Ups 'n' downs:** One steep/very steep ascent and descent (320 in 2200 m); one moderate ascent (110 in 1800 m); one moderate descent (160 in 2000 m)

♦ **Start:** Parking area at the junction of McPhails Fire Trail and Jacks Corner Rd, Kangaroo Valley. If travelling from Mittagong, turn west (right) off the main Kangaroo Valley Rd into Jacks Corner Rd, 500 m before Hampton Bridge (signpost says 'Bendeela Picnic Area'). The parking area is 1½ km past Bendeela Pondage, on the right.

TRACK NOTES

We recommend wearing slacks or over-pants because of stinging nettles in one small patch.

♦ From the parking area take the trail north and up the first of several steep climbs through tall eucalypt forest vegetation which includes the interesting Hybrid Blue Gum. The track going off to right at ❶ cuts off a little distance but is very steep. Just beyond the top of the escarpment, the track to Mount Carrialoo (marked by a cairn) goes off to the left ❷. The fire trail veers right.

♦ The trail passes around the base of Mount Carrialoo, turns north-east and descends gently into a clearing ❸. From here the trail narrows slightly and climbs steadily to a signposted intersection ❹. Take the left-hand fork, but note that you will return to this point via the right-hand track. About 1½ km of moderate climbing will bring you to the gravel road ❺, which services the Kangaroo (water) Pipeline.

♦ Turn south (right) at the road and follow it to where it curves south-east (left) after a downhill stretch of about 500 m. At the beginning of a roadside

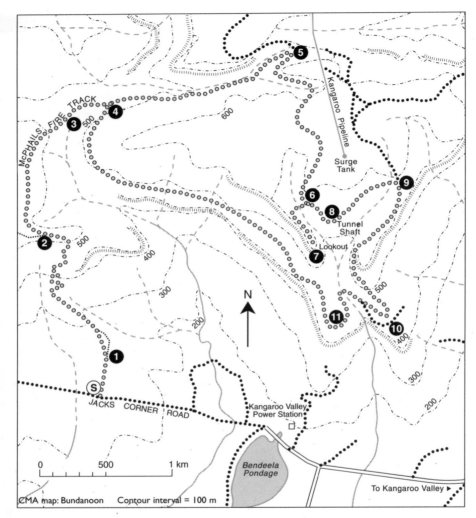

barrier, a rough track goes off to the south-west (right) ❻. Follow this track for about 400 m, as far as the cliff edge ❼ 🍎. The track is indistinct in places but the white-and-red underground cable markers are a good guide. The cliff edge affords beautiful views of Kangaroo Valley, Bendeela Pondage and Mount Carrialoo. From the same spot, it is possible to observe the tiered

nature of the ridges above the valley, a reflection of the inter-bedding of Permian sandstones and conglomerates (the cliffs) and softer rocks (the slopes).

◆ Return to the road, turn south-east (right) and proceed on past the shaft of the Kangaroo Pipeline ❽, under the power lines to the road intersection at ❾. Turn south (right) and follow the road along and down through the cliff line and under the power lines again. Stay with the road as it descends steeply to the cleared site of an old farm **10**. The road to the west (right) from the farm is grassed over at first but becomes clearer — although overgrown with stinging nettles in patches. Beyond the site of some old huts **11**, the track goes north-west before swinging north to its junction with McPhails Fire Trail at **4**. At the junction turn left for the return walk to the car park.

Bracken, *Pteridium esculentum*

Index

Page numbers in italics refer to photos, figures and illustrations

Index